The Ethnic Press

This book is part of the Peter Lang Media and Communication list.
Every volume is peer reviewed and meets
the highest quality standards for content and production.

PETER LANG
New York • Washington, D.C./Baltimore • Bern
Frankfurt • Berlin • Brussels • Vienna • Oxford

LEARA D. RHODES

The Ethnic Press
SHAPING THE AMERICAN DREAM

PETER LANG
New York • Washington, D.C./Baltimore • Bern
Frankfurt • Berlin • Brussels • Vienna • Oxford

Library of Congress Cataloging-in-Publication Data

Rhodes, Leara.
The ethnic press: shaping the American dream / Leara D. Rhodes.
p. cm.
Includes bibliographical references and index.
1. Ethnic press—United States—History.
2. American newspapers—Foreign language press.
3. American periodicals—Foreign language press.
4. Immigrants—United States. I. Title.
PN4884.R57   071'.3089—dc22   2010023344
ISBN 978-1-4331-1038-2 (hardcover)
ISBN 978-1-4331-1037-5 (paperback)

Bibliographic information published by **Die Deutsche Nationalbibliothek**.
Die Deutsche Nationalbibliothek lists this publication in the "Deutsche
Nationalbibliografie"; detailed bibliographic data is available
on the Internet at http://dnb.d-nb.de/.

FSC

Mixed Sources

Product group from well-managed
forests, controlled sources and
recycled wood or fiber

Cert no. SCS-COC-002464
www.fsc.org
©1996 Forest Stewardship Council

The paper in this book meets the guidelines for permanence and durability
of the Committee on Production Guidelines for Book Longevity
of the Council of Library Resources.

To

Jessica Ben Palumbo

Contents

Acknowledgments

This research was encouraged by the Anam Cara Writer's and Artist's Retreat; John Lent of Temple University; and Jessica Ben Palumbo, Esq.

Part I / Overview

"Ethnic press," as used here, is defined and placed within the context of immigration history and the functions of the press. How the ethnic press may have helped shape the American Dream is the argument made through historical examples. This is not a history book, though history is used to track the dream. The American Dream was first articulated from the immigrants' perspective with J. Hector St. John de Crevecoeur's "Letters from an American Farmer 1782." James Truslow Adams wrote in *The Epic of America* (1931, p. 404): "The American Dream is that dream of a land in which life should be better and richer and fuller for everyone, with opportunity for each according to ability or achievement." Other writers have described the American Dream as a religious paradise, or racial equality. As immigrants came to America with the American Dream pulling them from their homelands, the dream changed from one of paradise and wealth to one of economic independence and opportunity. As the immigrants assimilated into the American culture, they did not always settle for just the American way of life, they kept their homeland cultures alive with newspapers printing news in the home language and promoting homeland culture.

Chapter One / Introduction

Millions of people have come to America seeking a different life than the one they had in their home country. The storied lives of these immigrants fill copious volumes of literature, each volume with its own interpretation of history. The argument in this work is that by using examples of the history of immigrants in America as viewed through newspapers with immigrant readers, yet another interpretation can be made: How ethnic presses in America helped to shape the American Dream. Moreover, the press continues to reshape this dream as the function of the ethnic press has changed from one of acculturation to assimilation to cultural pluralism targeted at the immigrant audience. The similarities of the presses, whether they were sojourner, political, religious, or literary in form, add another interpretation to how the American Dream was shaped.

Definition of Ethnic Press

Literature includes countless books written about ethnic presses, defined here as a newspaper or other periodical created for a specific audience based on nationality, religion, and language. Ethnic presses historically have helped with immigrant assimilation into American culture, but these presses have had a primary focus of creating an old world community in the new world through language maintenance, cultural emphasis, religion, and political discussions. The terms used throughout literature include ethnic press, ethnic media, and foreign-language press. Whereas foreign-language press implies a language other than English is used, ethnic press can include those using both English and other languages. Thus the Irish, British, Australian, and some Caribbean and African presses in America constitute ethnic presses. Ethnic media refer to multiple platforms: newspaper, broadcast, Internet, etc. The ethnic press, as defined here, is limited to newspapers and printed publications.

Parameters

In this discussion, the ethnic press is defined as serving voluntary immigrants to the United States, a definition that does not include groups such as Native Americans and African Americans—who by their unique historical experience will not be addressed here. The Native American and early African American presses were created to establish a national voice for their people. They were not interested in assimilation, acculturation, or cultural pluralism. Each of these presses wanted a national spirit, a united front against the other people living in America at the time. The African American newspapers expressed abolitionist sentiment. Barbara K. Henritze's book, *Bibliographic Checklist of African American Newspapers* (1995), contains a complete checklist of African American newspapers since 1827 for a total of 5,539. Simmons (1998) writes in his preface that 3,000 black newspapers were published in the United States since 1827. Simmons recorded another 4,000 since his study began in 1981. The sheer volume of newspapers increases the necessity to write about the African American press separately from other newspapers of the period.

Whereas the African American newspapers gave a voice to the African Americans, the native newspapers were a source of information about sovereignty for Native Americans (Loew & Mella, 2005). The American Native Press Archives, one of the world's largest repositories of native thought, is a clearinghouse for information on American Indian and Alaska Native newspapers and periodicals and is housed in the Ottenheimer Library at the University of Arizona.

Though many Hispanics have entered the country voluntarily, many were here long before the country was settled. Félix Gutiérrez found news in the Americas produced in a booklet "hoja volante," by Juan Rodriquez in 1541, nearly 150 years before the first English colony newspaper (cited in Mendoza, 2009, para 3). The large volume of media targeted at Hispanics would overwhelm a single volume; therefore, their presses will not be discussed here either.

All three of these groups: Native Americans, African Americans, and Hispanics need their own volumes to give their vast history the importance they deserve. Instead, this work will concentrate on how the ethnic press targeting immigrants who came to America as volunteers may have contributed in significant ways to the immigrant experience and to the legacy these presses may have left within the United States in shaping the American Dream. Many people left countries from all over the world, going to England, Australia, Canada, and America. In this work only those immigrants coming to America will be included. The story begins with the colonial period and stops with the aftermath of September 11, 2001. The events of 9/11 changed how immigrants enter the United States, and therefore that date is a logical place to stop and reassess what the American Dream may be in the future.

Immigration Phases

Different phases of immigration and the development of ethnic presses have been identified in literature. These phases are significant to this discussion because they link the development of the ethnic press with that of shaping the American Dream. By tracking immigration, similarities of the ethnic presses can be highlighted. The first phase began in the colonial period up to the 1860s. Ten million immigrants settled in the United States. Immigrant groups visible during this time came from England, Ireland, Germany, France, Scandinavia, the Netherlands, and China.

A second phase was between the years of 1865 and 1890. The Civil War in the United States had ended. Wars in Europe had ended (the Napoleonic wars; the wars of Prussia against Denmark, Austria, and France between 1864 and 1871) and soldiers returned to overburdened farmlands. Free land grants after 1865 in the United States appealed to these landless people. The Industrial Revolution, expansion of the West with the railroads, and the gold rushes encouraged people to come to America while laws in Eastern Europe that created state religions pushed many religious people such as the Mennonites, Herrnhüteres, Pietists, Baptists, and German Quakers to leave. Ten million more immigrants came to America, and there were 796 ethnic presses by 1886 (Park, 1922).

The peak of the ethnic press came in 1907 during the third phase with the "open door" immigration policy of the United States from 1900 to 1930. Many immigrants were arriving from central and Eastern Europe. Twenty-two million immigrants came to America between the years of 1890 and 1930. They were Austro-Hungarian, Turkish, Lithuanian, Russian, Jewish, Greek, Italian, and Romanian. By 1920 there were 1,052 ethnic presses in the United States, and between 1884 and 1920 more than 3,444 newspapers were started (Park, 1922).

A fourth phase developed between the 1930s and the 1980s. American quota legislation and the aging of the first generation of immigrants in America was a period of decline in immigration. Layered within the fourth phase, though, was a revival in the 1960s of immigration issues as displaced persons and political refugees were entering the United States after wars in Asia and Latin America. These immigrants were more educated than the previous generations, creating a brain drain of intellectuals and skilled people from these areas. These political refugees were often singled out by the ethnic presses as the stories told within their pages focused on the home country problems and served as a way to keep immigrants informed. This 1960s revival coincided with the civil rights movement and offered ethnic communities cohesion, a shared identity, and pride.

At the turn of the 21st century, the fifth phase began. More wars, more famine, and tighter immigration laws after September 11, 2001, changed the patterns of immigrants entering the United States. Many of the issues connected with immigration in the first 10 years of the new century concern illegal immigration (centering on Hispanics), asylum seeking (such as the Cuban vs. the Haitian boat people), and refugees from Bosnia, Sudan, and Iraq.

Justification of Why the Ethnic Press Should Be Studied

The invention of the printing press opened up new channels of communication. Newspapers began as an information gathering and dissemination medium and morphed into an agent for change and one that assimilated large groups of immigrants into the American culture. This is where this work starts—discussing the development of the ethnic press in the United States from its early functions of acculturation through its function of assimilation and then its function of cultural pluralism.

Most books on ethnic presses concentrate on one language or nationality. R.E. Park (1922), in his much quoted book *Immigrant Press and Its Control,* suggested that the reason for so few studies on the ethnic press was that there were so many languages and that the presses must be treated separately.   However, J. Zubrzycki, in his article "The Role of the Foreign-Language Press in Migrant Integration" in *Population Studies*

(1958), argued that most ethnic newspapers had five major divisions: news of the country of settlement, world news, home-country news, group life and interests, and editorial features. The way news was divided and the amount of space dedicated to certain topics was seen to be directly related to the intensity of the ethnic group's nationalistic feelings.

Following Park's argument, this work takes the approach that there are differences among ethnic presses such as the cultures, languages, and issues, which make each press significantly different from another; however, following Zubrzycki's argument, there are similarities as to how immigrants have used newspapers as sojourners, proponents of political issues, for religious education and unity, and for literary enlightenment. There are rationales for why the presses targeted certain audiences and the problems these ethnic presses endured. Through the newspaper, a public sphere was created. Jürgen Habermas defines the public sphere:

> By the public sphere we mean first of all a realm of our social life in which something approaching a public opinion can be formed. Access is guaranteed to all citizens. A portion of the public sphere comes into being in every conversation in which private individuals assemble to form a public body....Citizens behave as a public body when they confer in an unrestricted fashion—that is, with the guarantee of freedom of assembly and association and the freedom to express and publish their opinions—about matters of general interest. In a large public body this kind of communication requires specific means of transmitting information and influencing those who receive it. Today newspapers and magazines, radio and TV are the media of the public sphere. (1974, p. 49)

Immigrants learned that a newspaper was essential to both urban and rural life. Many of the immigrants coming early to America were illiterate. Having the newspaper read to them was a luxury. However, wanting to have a better life forced the issue of education and literacy. A person needed to understand the issues in order to be a more productive citizen in this new country of America. This work approaches the development of the ethnic press in the United States as shaping the American Dream through its functions of acculturation, assimilation, and cultural pluralism. As the immigrant population settled, the functions of the ethnic press changed to maintain and yet attract new markets and audiences. Thus, by redefining how the ethnic press is studied, then maybe something can be gleaned about how people have learned to live together with all their differences. This work asks what is important about the ethnic press in order for us to understand how people have come to live and to work in America. And, how has the ethnic press recorded the movement from immigrant populations moving from acculturation to assimilation to cultural pluralism by shaping the American Dream?

Chapter Development

Part I gives an overview of all the chapters in this book. The overview section begins with this introduction. Chapter Two identifies the larger socio-cultural realm of the ethnic press. There were major social problems in America, and these affected the ethnic presses. Quotas limited the number of people entering the country. Discriminatory legislation and unfair treatment of immigrants created concentration camps for the Japanese on the West Coast and limited where the Irish could live and work. Included are the legislations of the 1920s and the anti-ethnic sentiments against the Chinese, Japanese, Jewish, Irish, Italians, and Germans.

Chapter Three defines the ethnic press and places it in a historical period of immigration and immigration laws. This chapter identifies the immigrant in terms of the American Dream and investigates how communities developed, how immigrants established identities, and offers an explanation as to why the press was important to so many different audiences and what distinguished the ethnic presses from those of mainstream society. The role of the immigrant editors and journalists within the community played an important part in linking the immigrants with their home countries.

Chapter Four describes the functions of the ethnic press with examples from the Irish, Jewish, Scandinavian, Chinese, Lithuanian presses, as well as the socialist and anarchist presses and trade union publications. These ethnic presses fostered language maintenance, cultivated ethnic pride, tied the community together socially, and nourished a sense of identification and survival for the people. The editors of the ethnic presses redefined the functions of their presses as their audiences changed. These ethnic presses also took part in working out misunderstandings and easing fears between the immigrants and the native-born

Americans. Some presses, like the Russian and Irish, helped search for missing people to reunite families and settle disputes.

Part II of the book focuses on missions and motivations of the presses. Though the presses serving ethnic communities often were language specific related to the home country, these presses had a mission for existing and were motivated by their editors as being a sojourner, religious, political, or literary press. Chapter Five examines the sojourner mentality with presses that targeted people who came to America but ultimately wanted to return to their home country. Many immigrants had planned to stay only long enough to make money to go back home to buy a farm or to invest in a business. Examples are given from the Hungarian, Japanese, and Chinese presses. Other sojourners included political activists, refugees, asylum seekers, and exiles. Modern sojourners would include employees of international organizations, guest workers, students, entertainers, and diplomats.

Chapter Six focuses on the ethnic press that targeted people who came to America because of religious persecution or who were united in the new American communities through their churches. These immigrants brought with them the religious differences that existed in their home country. Controversies surrounding religion included how labor issues were religiously supported, how language-specific religious education caused tensions, and how the anti-Catholic movement fueled pages in the ethnic press.

Political press issues are discussed in Chapter Seven, as many immigrants left their home country because of political persecution. Party newspapers developed to continue the fight for freedom of the home country. The political presses were concerned with the fate of the home country and often debated the group's national identity. These presses were used to foster nationalism. Examples include revolutionary presses of the German Forty-Eighters, the Chinese system, Lithuanian and Sicilian militancy, Danish and Norwegian labor and party newspapers, and the Young Ireland's rebellion newspapers. The ethnic press was heavily involved in American politics as a way of influencing immigrant issues. Then as a war began, the ethnic press would take a stand against U.S. policy, such as the Irish, Lebanese, Italians, Germans, Czechs, and Hungarians. The newspapers spoke out against immigration restrictions and used propaganda to espouse nationalistic views. The section on labor presses includes the anarchist and socialist presses.

Chapter Eight follows how some presses were more interested in voicing opinions and discussing ideas than they were in disseminating the news. These presses published belles-lettres and essays. Some reproduced and serialized literary classics. In the 1960s, the third and fourth generations began to seek more heritage and cultural linkages through these presses. These include the Chinese, Czechs, Germans, Hungarian, Jewish/Yiddish, Swedish, and Lithuanians. Calendars were an important contribution of the literary presses.

The last section of this work discusses the challenges and future of the ethnic presses. Chapter Nine examines the fundamental internal issues encountered by the ethnic presses. These included illiteracy, indifference, and lack of leisure time of the targeted audiences. Rivalries existed between newspapers within the same ethnic group. Other hindrances of the press included competition from other media, outmoded equipment, and economic problems.

The next to the last chapter of the book, Chapter Ten, moves the time line of the ethnic press from one of acculturation to assimilation to cultural pluralism. Diversity issues and the importance being placed on ethnic consciousness makes knowing about how ethnic presses have functioned significantly. What can be learned about how people live together is paramount to a better understanding of the world. The chapter uses definitions of integration, assimilation, separation, and marginalization to discuss cultural identity, concluding with the process of assimilation and the role of media. Chapter Eleven summarizes what has been learned about ethnic presses in terms of how media are used by new populations entering the United States. The chapter discusses how media continue to redefine themselves when targeting new markets and how immigrants want to shape the American Dream with their own life stories.

Chapter Two / Larger Socio-Cultural Change

A newspaper is a device for making
the ignorant more ignorant and the crazy crazier.
H.L. Mencken (1949)

Ethnic newspapers taught immigrants about the host society. Through the ethnic presses, the earlier stage of providing information to assist the immigrants through the process of assimilation has traditionally been the function of newspapers. Many immigrants were illiterate, only able to converse in their home country's language, and were alienated from the American society through discrimination and prejudices. Therefore, what they did learn about America was through the lens of the ethnic press and through the culture of their ethnic enclaves. Their children were raised to have a certain worldview. Sociologists argue that social interaction plays a fundamental role in the development of cognition that all the higher functions originate as actual relationships between individuals (Vygotsky, 1978). To understand the immigrant, then, we must also examine the external social world in which that individual has developed. Through language, children and other novices in a society obtain knowledge of how the society functions and how they should interact within that society. Social interactions are fundamentally cultural, and language plays a significant role in the culture (Ochs, 1986).

What was the immigrants' world like? Did they find the American Dream? Did successes and money flow to them and their children and alleviate all worries? The reality was that though success and wealth did happen to a few, the majority of immigrants were faced with financial hardships, social isolation through prejudices and exclusions, and loneliness based on their memories of home. These forced immigrants to live in ethnic communities, where they could establish a network of institutions and associations that allowed them to function within an environment they knew through culture and language. The overcrowding of the tenements, poverty, crime, and the separation of families all contributed to the immigrant losing the American Dream.

Prejudices against immigrants often were a reaction to various downturns in the economy. Americans felt that immigrants were taking jobs from citizens. Other anti-immigrant prejudices were a combination of economic and ethnic prejudices. The Japanese and German prejudices resulted from the world wars. The other anti-foreign sentiments evolved from education status and class status. Americans thought that the Chinese, Irish, and Italians were below them and should not become part of the American society. The early Chinese, Irish, and Italian immigrants were uneducated, unskilled, rural laborers. Religious prejudices against the Catholics and Jews were deeply expressed and have lasted many generations. Along with identifying the prejudices against certain immigrant groups, there were laws passed to isolate the immigrant; physical harm and death came to many others.

Late 19th century anti-immigrant sentiment soared in the United States. There was an economic depression and immigrants were blamed for taking Americans' jobs. Racialist theories circulated in the press, advancing pseudoscientific theories that alleged that Mediterranean types were inherently inferior to people of northern European heritage. Drawings and songs caricaturing the new immigrants as childlike, criminal, or subhuman became commonplace. One cartoon in the 1800s claimed that if immigration was properly restricted, Americans would never be troubled with anarchism, socialism, and the Mafia. The *Newburyport Herald* published the following report:

> Nearly two thousand English and Irish immigrants have arrived in the United States, within these few weeks. It is hoped, President Jefferson, on the meeting of Congress, will repeat to that body what he says on the subject in the "Notes on Virginia;" and call its attention to remedying the growing evil. (1801, p. 2)[1]

Whereas businessmen saw the need to have a foreign workforce to keep wages low and profits high, when these foreign laborers became the leaders of organized labor, the businessmen as well as the native-born American workers reacted negatively. Workers saw the immigrants taking away their jobs. In 1886, a Midwestern carpenter cried out: "We poor native-born citizens are just pulled around as dogs by foreign people. We do not stand any show, and it seems as though everything is coming to the very worst in the near future unless free immigration is stopped" (Higham, 2002, p. 47).

This economic downturn with a surplus of labor would lead to tensions when unemployment was severe. This was evident when the mining industry shut down operations and a large number of people were left unemployed. These work-related tensions resulted in passing of legislation to restrict immigration and to hasten citizenship. In the Revenue Act of 1818, Congress imposed on non-resident aliens an income tax twice as heavy as that for citizens and resident aliens so that thousands of foreign workers declared their intentions to become citizens. Immigrants were restricted from construction of public works if not declaring to become a citizen in 1886 through a bill passed in the U.S. House of Representatives (Jillson, 2004). Several state legislatures adopted such legislation, and Illinois, Wyoming, and Idaho prohibited corporations from hiring any alien who had not declared his or her intention to become a citizen and banned non-declaring aliens from both state and municipal projects in 1889 (Rolle, 1999).

The ethnic press warned against the worsening of legislation against immigrants (Fishman & Nahimy, 1966). They were right; new discriminatory laws were passed. In 1906 a new attempt to pass a literacy test for incoming immigrants was only narrowly defeated. In 1908 aliens were required to pay $20 to obtain a hunting license while citizens only paid $1 (Hays, 1957/1995). And in 1909 Michigan prohibited the issuance of a barber's license to any foreigner (Higham, 2002). Anti-immigrant sentiment continued until the 1920s, when severe restrictions on immigration were put into place by the U.S. Congress. These anti-immigrant sentiments were used in the mainstream press and refuted in the ethnic presses. Examples used here are of anti-foreign sentiments against the Chinese, Japanese, Jewish, Irish, Italians, and Germans.

Anti-Chinese

The Chinese came to California in the first place as sojourners. They came to make money and then return home. China imposed harsh treatment for any immigrant who wanted to return: They would be arrested and decapitated, but Chinese rural laborers came any way. Then the Burlingame-Seward Treaty of 1868 formalized the Chinese central government's recognition that Chinese could legally migrate to the United States (Lee, 1988). Anson Burlingame was an American diplomat hired by the Chinese to protect their interests in the United States. This treaty did not lessen the hatred against the Chinese in the 1870s and 1880s, which included lynching, boycotts, and mass expulsions. The California legislature ratified an article in their constitution in 1879, forbidding any corporation to employ directly or indirectly any Chinese or Mongolian. This article was struck down as unconstitutional, but not before the press debated the issue at great length (Lee, 1988).

Chinese immigrants had to deal with the threat of armed attackers. Americans exploited and ridiculed the Chinese. A Chinese man was beaten by an American while waiting for a bus; both went to court and the American was fined $10.[2] A jury acquitted the killers of two Chinese men after a 30-minute deliberation in Washington territory. Tacoma residents forced Chinese from their homes onto the prairie in winter (Huntzicker, 1995). Historian B.L. Sung (1971) wrote that murdering Chinese became such a commonplace occurrence that the newspapers seldom bothered to print the stories. Police officials winked at the attacks, and politicians all but incited more of the same. There were thousands of cases of murder, robbery, and assault, but only two or three instances where the guilty were brought to justice (Sung, 1971).

The Chinese were harassed by punitive laws and regulations, targeted solely at them. The Foreign Miners' License Tax law required all non-native born workers to pay the exorbitant rate of $20 per month for the right to mine.[3] The Sidewalk Ordinance of 1870 banned the Chinese method of carrying vegetables and laundry on a pole. There was hostility in the mining regions in 1871 with violence in Chinatown in Los Angeles. In San Francisco, the Queue Ordinance of 1873 outlawed the wearing of long braids by men, a Chinese custom. Americans for fun would jump a Chinese man and cut off his queue. The queue symbolized loyalty to his country and his plan to return home. Loss of this hair would be evidence of an intention to emigrate and would mean death if he returned to China (McCunn, 1979). Other ordinances prohibited Chinese immigrants from working for federal, state, and local governments, and their children could not be educated in public schools. For several decades, a law was in place that prevented Chinese immigrants from testifying in court against Americans of European descent—effectively placing thousands of immigrants outside the protection of the law (Parks, 1995).

In 1878, a labor organization warned against the damaging effects of Chinese businesses.

> Men from China come here to do laundry work. The China Empire contains six hundred million inhabitants. The supply of these men is inexhaustible. Every one doing this work takes bread from the mouths of our women. So many have come of late, that to keep at work, they're obliged to cut prices. (Huntzicker, 1995, p. 97)

The Chinese were willing to take any job, yet their livelihoods were much better off than when they were in warring, starving China. The Chinese were often baffled that the white worker disliked the Chinese who would work for any price. The *Chinese Newspaper* reported an incident where a factory fired all the white American workers and hired Chinese workers. The salaries were low; the Chinese asked for more but the owners refused. The newspaper seemed puzzled that the white workers should be angry at the Chinese willingness to work for less. Meanwhile, the white workers threatened to burn down Chinese homes (Huntzicker, 1995). In other work-related disturbances, the homes were burned and the Chinese were killed. In Rock Springs, Wyoming, in 1885, a fight erupted between the Chinese and whites. A mob banished two foremen, took their guns, and marched into Chinatown. They burned buildings and shot any Chinese they saw, killing 28, wounding 15, and causing property damage worth $150,000. The riot captured national attention and was covered in *Harper's Weekly* and *Frank Leslie's Illustrated Newspaper* (Huntzicker, 1995). The *Rock Springs Inde-*

pendent adopted a slogan: "The Chinese must go." Mob violence against the Chinese increased throughout the West, and the Chinese sought refuge in urban San Francisco (Huntzicker, 1995).

In 1882, Congress passed the Chinese Exclusion Act, restricting immigration from China under penalty of imprisonment and deportation. It also made Chinese immigrants permanent aliens by excluding them from U.S. citizenship. Chinese men in the United States now had little chance of ever reuniting with their wives, or of starting families in their new home. These restrictions forced the Chinese immigrants to live a life apart, and to build a society in which they could survive on their own. After 1882, only Chinese merchants, students, diplomats, and temporary travelers came to the United States (Lee, 1988).

Reforms were needed. Editorials in the Chinese-language newspapers published in Hawaii and San Francisco in 1898 repeatedly called for constitutional and progressive social and economic reforms. They argued that China's stature in the international community and the Chinese immigrants' status in America were intimately related (Lee, 1988). The *Chinese Newspaper* also covered hate groups. The newspaper objected to political groups attacking Chinese workers and those who boycotted businesses hiring Chinese workers (Huntzicker, 1995). The *San Francisco China News* criticized customs officials for destroying people's clothes while searching their luggage. The newspaper advised readers that police could not hold them without allowing a call to a friend or relative and that if they failed to follow the rule, the policeman could be fined $50 or be fired (Huntzicker, 1995). In an article about new immigrants, the *San Francisco China News* reported that a boat arrived with 90 Chinese women, 22 of whom appeared to be young. The police said the women looked like prostitutes and asked them to go to the police station. The boat's captain took offense, but the women were detained for trial. The newspaper advocated a speedy trial because the women were becoming sick and hysterical (Huntzicker, 1995).

The Chinese were so mistreated in America that other ethnic groups were motivated to speak out. For example, the *Irish World* criticized a bill to outlaw Chinese immigration and accused U.S. senators of

...loading their debates with race-bigotry while the Great Disinherited of all races are forced, by the infernal economic system which obtains in this and other lands, to perish miserably....We have no feeling of ill-will toward the Chinaman. He is a man endowed by the Creator with certain "inalienable rights." And his rights are as sacred as the American's, the Irishman's and the German's, or any other man of any other nationality.[4]

Anti-Japanese

The Chinese Exclusion Act also affected the Japanese, but it was the 1907 Gentlemen's Agreement with Japan that placed more limits on Asian workers and their families from immigrating to the United States. The Gentlemen's Agreement was an informal agreement between Japan and the United States in which Japan agreed to halt unrestricted emigration of its citizens to the United States. In return, the United States promised to stop discrimination against the Japanese, thus ending its segregation of Asian children in San Francisco schools. The American Federation of Labor supported immigration restriction. In 1920, Californians denied Japanese newcomers the right to own land. Later, the 1952 McCarren-Walter Act placed all immigrants of Asian ancestry under a new quota of 2,000 immigrants annually for all 19 countries of the Asia-Pacific triangle. The anti-Japanese sentiments gained momentum with the incarceration of 120,000 West Coast Japanese Americans after Pearl Harbor was attacked by the Japanese during World War II.

Hours after the attack, prominent Japanese Americans were arrested by U.S. security personnel. Arrested were businessmen, journalists, teachers, and civic officials. The press published virulent attacks on the Japanese Americans, calling them spies, saboteurs, and enemy agents. Fanning this wave of hysteria was Executive Order 9066 issued by President Roosevelt in February 1942. This Executive Order authorized the U.S. military to evacuate any and all persons from military areas and to provide accommodations for them elsewhere. The Civilian Exclusion Orders were issued by the army in March and required that all Japanese persons, both alien and non-alien, be evacuated and confined to relocation camps farther inland. This order declared that all of California, Washington, and Oregon were military areas. More than 100,000 Japanese Americans were uprooted and transferred thousands of miles away from home. By the end of the war, 125,000 people, half of them children, had spent time in these internment camps.

All of the Japanese internment camps had newspapers published during World War II, 1942–1945. These newspapers documented the lifestyles in the camps as well as any personal involvement in the war. The newspapers included:

o   *Colorado Times* (Denver, Colo.)
o   *Communique* (Denson, Ark.)
o   *Denson Tribune* (Denson, Ark.)
o   *Gila News-Courier* (Rivers, Ariz.)
o   *Granada Bulletin* (Amache, Colo.)
o   *Granada Pioneer* (Amache, Colo.)
o   *Manzanar Free Press* (Manzanar, Calif.)
o   *Minidoka Irrigator* (Hunt, Idaho)
o   *Newell Star* (Newell, Calif.)
o   *Official Daily Press Bulletin* (Poston, Ariz.)
o   *Poston Chronicle* (Poston, Ariz.)
o   *Rocky Shimpo* (Denver, Colo.)
o   *Rohwer Outpost* (Rohwer, Ark.)
o   *Rohwer Relocator* (McGehee, Ark.)
o   *Santa Anita Pacemaker* (Santa Anita, Calif.)
o   *Tanforan Totalizer* (San Bruno, Calif.)
o   *Topaz Times* (Topaz, Utah)
o   *Tule Lake WRA* center information bulletin (Newell, Calif.)
o   *Tulean Dispatch* (Newell, Calif.)
o   *Heart Mountain Sentinel* (Heart Mountain, Wyo.)

In 1942, Bill Hosokawa began the *Heart Mountain Sentinel* to keep the 10,000 people in the community informed. He had to leave his home in Seattle and report to the Heart Mountain internment camp in Wyoming. His wife and son moved with him. Heart Mountain was a one-square-mile compound with barracks, guarded by soldiers. The War Relocation Authority (WRA) began searching for people to start weekly newspapers. Before coming to the internment camp, Hosokawa had launched a small English-language newspaper in Singapore and also worked overseas for the *Shanghai Times* and a business magazine, the *Far Eastern Review*. (Hosokawa, 1998)

The first issue of the *Sentinel* was published on October 24, 1942. Among the staffers were Haruo Imura, the paper's managing editor, who had worked for Japanese American newspapers in San Francisco, and Louise Suski, the city editor, who came from the *Rafu Shimpo*, a Japanese paper in Los Angeles. Most of the staff had little or no reporting experience. Paid a monthly wage of $16, they used a converted military barracks as their office; this amounted to a single room 20 feet wide and 120 feet long with only a few benches and tables. There was no printing press, so the first issue was a mimeographed newsletter notifying residents of weather forecasts and where to go for medical services. Eventually, Hosokawa worked out a deal with the *Cody Enterprise*, another weekly newspaper in the area, to have the *Sentinel* published on their equipment (Hosokawa, 1998). They printed 7,000 copies, which were distributed free to residents.

The *Sentinel* was established, funded, and monitored by the WRA, as were all the other camp papers. Beyond the threat of government censorship, the staff of the *Sentinel* also had to contend with their own hesitation to report on some issues. The military draft, for instance, divided the camp. There were resisters, but there were also the flag-waving Japanese Americans. The newspaper published articles praising the Japanese American soldiers who were fighting the Japanese. The newspaper also played down the coverage of cultural Japanese traditions (Hosokawa, 1998).

When a barbed-wire fence was erected around the camp, the *Sentinel* found its first big story. The camp was in the desert. The newspaper published an article explaining why camp occupants opposed the fence. If the government insisted the fence was for their protection, the paper noted, why were the guns of the watchtower guards pointed inside rather than out? Under Hosokawa's leadership, the staff of the *Sentinel* tried to balance their obligation to report objectively with their desire to fight for their rights and those of their community (1998). The content of the paper reflected that the readers were trying to cope with being imprisoned without a trial, with the loss of their democratic freedoms, and with the depression caused by camp life.

As the war against Japan raged on, the U.S. government demanded that all Japanese Americans in the camps sign loyalty oaths or be imprisoned or deported. Yet, even after signing, the Japanese Americans remained in the camps and the males faced being drafted even though their basic rights had been denied. Many resisted and were imprisoned. Other residents kept up a façade of innocent ignorance, but mocked the barrack directors and prison guards and called them blockheads behind their backs (Hosokawa, 1998).

In such a volatile atmosphere, Hosokawa's newspaper offered a voice of calm defiance. "The *Sentinel* had a dual responsibility. It had to give voice to its readers' anger, supporting their demands for justice and providing articulate leadership, but it also had to be cautious about fueling the anger of citizens' unjustly imprisoned," Hosokawa writes in his book *Out of the Frying Pan*. To achieve the middle ground was difficult, and the balance was often precarious (Hosokawa & Noel, 1998). Hosokawa's newspaper sought to help its readers cope with the circumstances of their new life. It offered information on the war and national affairs. It helped bring the community together by providing a forum for its readers for a reasoned discussion. People were encouraged to write in and complain about conditions or make suggestions for improving life in the camp. One of the complaints was that there was not enough coal to keep the barracks warm.

The *Sentinel* also reported news. Whereas the mainstream newspapers were feeding racial prejudices against Japanese Americans, the *Sentinel* tried to refute the charges. In October 1943, after a year of running the *Sentinel*, Hosokawa was released from the Heart Mountain camp. He and his family went to Des Moines, Iowa, where Hosokawa found a job as a copy editor for the city newspaper, the *Register*. Soon afterward, he joined the staff of *The Denver Post*. By the time he retired from journalism in 1993, Hosokawa had served as a Korean War correspondent, a Sunday magazine editor, an editorial-page editor, and a newspaper ombudsman.

In December 1944, the war emergency ended and internees were allowed to return to the West Coast beginning in early 1945. Each person was given $25 and a train ticket. By June 1945, only 2,000 people had left the Heart Mountain camp. Their reluctance to return to their original homes in California and

Washington was based on fears of racism they would face on the outside as well as the struggle of starting their lives over.

Wyoming pushed the internees out. To discourage Japanese Americans from remaining in the state, Wyoming passed laws that prevented them from owning land and voting. The effort was successful; the last trainload of internees left Heart Mountain on November 10, 1945. To start their lives over was difficult for most of the internees. However, one editor had an easier transition due in large part to the publisher's advance planning. Togo Tanaka, editor of the *Rafu Shimpo*, a Japanese-language newspaper in Little Tokyo, California, left the Manzanar (California) internment camp to revive the newspaper in 1946. The publisher, Akira Komai, had arranged for the newspaper's rent to be paid during the war and hid the Japanese type under the floorboard (Yokoi, 1993).

Anti-Jewish

Restrictive immigration laws during 1920–1924 limited visas available to immigrants from Europe to an amount equal to 3 percent of the 1910 census and allocated most of these visas to nationals from northwestern Europe. Excluded completely were Asians, as discussed earlier, and Jews.

Jews faced discrimination from the early colonial days in America. Twenty-three Portuguese Jews arrived from Brazil in 1654 to settle in New Amsterdam (New York). In an attempt to keep the Jews from staying, they were banned from public worship, buying land, holding public office, trading with Native Americans, working as craftsmen, or engaging in retail trade. The Jewish discrimination did not lessen as the years passed. In 1790, after the Bill of Rights, religious tests for holding public office were still held in Connecticut, Maryland, Massachusetts, South Carolina, Georgia, Rhode Island, North Carolina, and New Hampshire. The population of Jews was small until 1848, when the Jewish population increased to 50,000 as immigrants arrived from Russia. The increased number of Jews alarmed Protestant Americans, and negative stereotypes of Jews in newspapers, literature, drama, art, and popular culture grew more commonplace, and physical attacks became more frequent. The Civil War created more tensions for the American Jews, as reflected by the fact that Gen. Ulysses S. Grant issued General Order No. 11 on December 17, 1862, banishing all Jews from western Tennessee—an order that President Abraham Lincoln rescinded.[5]

By 1880, the Jewish population had increased to around 230,000. They faced an established system of social exclusion, discriminatory laws, and covenants. A public anti-Semitic example in 1877 was the exclusion of Joseph Seligman from the Grand Union Hotel in Saratoga Springs, New York. Seligman was a well-established, respected Jewish banker who had been offered the position of Secretary of Treasury by President Ulysses S. Grant for his contributions to the war effort. He refused the offer for reasons he did not disclose. Seligman, who was by now a celebrity, was denied a room because he was Jewish. Confident that his position in society, his near appointment as Secretary of Treasury of the United States, and his friendship with the president would give him clout, he publicized the anti-Semitic incident in local newspapers. To his shock, his complaints backfired. In response, newspapers published venomously anti-Semitic letters in support of keeping Jews out of Saratoga and other resorts. Soon many hotels posted "No Jews Admitted" signs. The Jewish community was stunned at first and later retaliated by purchasing a number of hotels in Saratoga (Jillson, 2004).

Immigration of Jews from Russia prompted the formation of American groups like the Immigration Restriction League, founded in 1894. These groups claimed that the new immigrants were culturally, intellectually, morally, and biologically inferior. By 1905, the Jewish population was 1.5 million, and rising prejudice prompted the formation of the American Jewish Committee and the Jewish fraternal group B'nai B'rith to set up the Anti-Defamation League to fight discrimination. Meanwhile the Ku Klux Klan called for "100 Percent Americanism" and white supremacy—no Jews allowed (Levitas, 1999).

A Midwest campaign against the Jews was launched by Henry Ford and was encouraged through the activities of the Ku Klux Klan. Ford bought the Dearborn Publishing Company and began the newspaper *The Dearborn Independent*. The newspaper first attacked Jews in its May 22, 1920, issue and continued to do so in 91 subsequent editions (Levitas, 1999). Having heard in advance about the plan to attack Jews, E.G. Pipp, editor of *The Dearborn Independent*, resigned in disgust in April 1920 and was replaced by William J. Cameron. Ford's personal secretary, Ernest Liebold, collected anti-Semitic material and passed this material to Cameron, who oversaw the articles, writing many of them himself. "When we get through with the Jews," Liebold was quoted in court as saying, "there won't be one of them who will dare raise his head in public" (Belth, 1979, p. 76).

During the first half of the 20th century, newspaper advertisements for resorts, jobs, and housing specified Christians only need apply. Employment discrimination became more pervasive in the years immediately before World War I, and quotas were placed on the number of Jews admitted to medical schools, colleges, and universities, first at Ivy League schools in the Northeast and then elsewhere (Levitas, 1999).

In the 1930s and 1940s, right-wing demagogues such as the Rev. Gerald L.K. Smith, Father Charles Coughlin, William Dudley Pelley, and the Rev. Gerald Winrod linked the Great Depression of the 1930s, the New Deal, President Franklin Roosevelt, and the threat of war in Europe to the machinations of an imagined international Jewish conspiracy that was both communist and capitalist. Smith, a Disciples of Christ minister, was the founder (1937) of the Committee of One Million and publisher (beginning in 1942) of *The Cross and the Flag*, a magazine that declared that "Christian character is the basis of all real Americanism." Coughlin was a Roman Catholic priest who endorsed the Protocols of the Elders of Zion and praised Nazi Germany. His weekly radio audience ranged between 5 million and 12 million listeners throughout the late 1930s, and his newspaper *Social Justice* reached 800,000 people at its peak in 1937, but was banned from the mail during the war. William Dudley Pelley founded (1933) the anti-Semitic Silvershirt Legion of America; nine years later he was convicted of sedition. Gerald Winrod, leader of Defenders of the Christian Faith, was eventually indicted for conspiracy to cause insubordination in the armed forces during World War II (Levitas, 1999).

Anti-Irish

In a popular quip of the day, as reported in the *Irish American*, a slave makes this observation: "My master is a great tyrant. He treats me as badly as if I were a common Irishman."[6]

The Irish were reviled because they were poor, foreign, and Catholic. They were so poor that when the military conscription law was passed, which exempted well-off males who could buy out their service, the Irish rioted with the worst riots in New York. For five days in July 1863, violence and looting took place, resulting in the deaths of 3 policemen, 105 rioters, 11 Africans, and one Native American (Mulcrone, 2003). In response to open hostility, the Irish moved deeper into imposed isolation. Their sense of exclusion and group consciousness intensified as they settled into the poorest parts of Boston and New York (Mulcrone, 2003).

American publishers fed the anti-Irish movement with gross characterizations. Thomas Nast's depictions in *Harper's Weekly* in New York of Irish politicians and clergy as grotesque ape-like monsters set an enduring standard in the 1870s through the 1890s for political cartoons and helped spur a nativist revival in the 1880s. Both the *Boston Pilot* and the *Irish World* condemned such depictions. *Harper's Weekly*, the *Irish World* lamented, "...constantly vilifies everything Irish American and Catholic."[7] Irish were seen as being loyal to priests. They were rowdy, impulsive, quarrelsome, drunken, and poor. "No Irish Need Apply" remained a common feature in job advertisements until the 1870s, mostly as a result of the Irish getting involved in local politics.

Anti-Italian

Italians were seen by Americans as illiterate with a propensity toward crime. Therefore, in 1891, when the New Orleans chief of police was found shot to death on the street, the mayor blamed "Sicilian gangsters" and rounded up more than 100 Sicilian Americans. Nineteen were put on trial and found not guilty for lack of evidence. A mob of 10,000 people, including many of New Orleans' most prominent citizens, broke into the jail. They dragged 11 Sicilians from their cells and lynched them, including two men jailed on other offenses (Gabaccia, 1988).

Italians worldwide were outraged. The Italian-language newspapers in the United States vigorously protested the abusive treatment of the Italians. The U.S. press generally approved of the lynching. It was the largest mass lynching in U.S. history.

Though many Italian-language newspapers responded to anti-Italian slurs in the American press and denounced references in the American press to Italian criminality, as World War I absorbed Italy into the conflict, the Italian radical press in the United States, which had been strong with hundreds of newspapers, was then suppressed. The Espionage Act was applied, as were the Trading with the Enemy Act and the Sedition Act. Editors of the radical press were consequently imprisoned or deported. For example, Luigi Galleani (1861–1931) was a major 20th century anarchist who was deported to Italy in 1919.

Famous among both Italians and Americans, Galleani was a proponent of propaganda by the deed. He was the founder and editor of the *Cronaca Sovversiva* (Subversive Chronicle), a major Italian-language anarchist periodical, which ran for a period of about 15 years before the American government shut it down. Historian Paul Avrich has described the newspaper, created on June 6, 1903, as "one of the most important and ably edited periodicals in the history of the anarchist movement" (1991, p. 50). With a circulation of 5,000, the newspaper was distributed in New York, New Jersey, and Massachusetts. While its circulation never exceeded 5,000, this periodical was of considerable influence within the movement and was read wherever there were Italian anarchists—from North and South America, Europe, to North Africa and Australia. In the United States the newspaper was circulated to newer immigrants and working class stonecutters, day laborers, and factory workers. Galleani was captured by authorities in 1906 after a socialist, Giacinto Menotti Serrati, editor of *Il Proletario* in New York, revealed Galleani's whereabouts in the wake of a lengthy personal dispute he had with him (Avrich, 1991).

Anti-German

The issue of what makes a press legitimate began when the American government questioned and challenged the substance of the German American collective consciousness expressed by the German-language press. Americans believed the German-language presses were not legitimate presses and were publishing German propaganda. Franklin D. Roosevelt in 1917 said, "Whatever may have been our judgment in normal times, we are convinced that today our most dangerous foe is the foreign-language press and every similar agency, such as the German-American Alliance, which holds the alien to his former associations and through them, to his former allegiance" ("Roosevelt Off for West," 1917, para. 2). Roosevelt in his active anti-German campaign advised his fellow citizens to shoot any German who showed himself disloyal. In 1913, Congress authorized the deportation of many aliens simply on grounds of belonging to an organization which advocated revolt or sabotage.

Vigilantism characterized the anti-German campaign throughout the nation. Children in St. Louis regularly stoned the delivery wagons of a German American grocery company. German American homes were smeared with yellow paint. A Wisconsin German American was ridden around on a rail after he claimed to be a pacifist. A German American in Florida received a flogging and was ordered to leave the state. German Americans who failed to demonstrate their loyalty often met threats of being tarred and feathered or hanged. Fervent "patriots" had no compunction about harassing, intimidating, or physically assaulting German Americans, since local and state officials rarely interceded to protect the rights of German Americans against these unjustified attacks. The Wilson administration intervened only when confronted with blatant violence, and then only reluctantly. Therefore, it was not surprising that state and local governments acquiesced, encouraged, and participated in the war against everything remotely German (Sonntag, 1994).

Each day a series of pro-German articles were written by people in the German Information Bureau, organized, financed, and directed by official representatives of Germany. These articles were compiled from the daily press, from German newspapers, German magazines, German books, and American books. The Bureau also courted the Irish American press and news service with the thought that if both the Irish and German people were against England, the two groups should work together. In April of 1915, the Bureau undertook the preparation and publication of an appeal to the American people. This appeal was published in most of the ethnic newspapers of the United States and in about 70 of the large daily papers published in the English language. The propaganda was handled by Louis N. Hammerling, president of the American Association of Foreign Language

Newspapers, an advertising agency of the ethnic press. Hammerling handed out advertising contracts and did business through the members and others who retained him for political and propaganda purposes. The American Association included 600–700 newspapers in 30 different languages exclusive of the German language with 6 million copies and 18 million readers. The newspapers printed anything Hammerling gave them. When in March 1915 Hammerling was asked to publish a piece to appeal to the American people against the manufacture and shipment of munitions to the Allies, Hammerling said he went into the proposition purely for profit (Sleeper, 1999). The appeal was as follows:

> We appeal to the American people, to the high-minded and courageous American press, and to the American manufacturer of powder, shrapnel, and cartridges, and we appeal to the workmen engaged in the plants devoted to the manufacture of ammunitions for use of the nations at war to immediately cease making powder, shrapnel, and cartridges destined to destroy our brothers, widow our sisters and mothers, and orphan their children, as well as destroy forever the priceless possession handed down by our ancestors....

> We appeal individually to the workmen of such factories, even at the sacrifice of their positions, to go on record as being unalterably opposed to being employed for the purpose of manufacturing ammunition to shatter the bodies and blot out the lives of their own blood relatives. (*New York Times*, 1918)[8]

Feeding the anti-German sentiment in America were the reports that German-language newspapers were publishing propaganda during the war years. The Bureau published an information sheet. Later George Sylvester Vierick would edit a weekly newspaper called the *Fatherland*, strongly pro-German with a wide circulation in the United States among Germans and German Americans. Dr. Bernard Dernberg supervised the publicity propaganda in the United States. He delivered lectures in different parts of the country and contacted men of prominence in literary and educational circles to enlist the efforts of newspaper representatives to give a favorable comment on the German cause. The Bureau purchased the *New York Evening Mail,* and Dr. Edward A. Rumley became managing editor. On November

13, 1920, the *New York Times* covered the trial of Rumley, who tried to hide the fact that funds to purchase the newspaper came from the German government.[9]

Of the more than 500 German-language periodicals that existed before the war, fewer than half were able to survive the war years. There were unsubstantiated claims of widespread German espionage and sabotage. Organizations of super patriots such as the National Security League harassed individuals, often with the connivance of state and local officials. Laws were passed banning the German language from schools and in some cases banning the use of any and all German books in school libraries. Publications such as Victor Berger's *Milwaukee Leader* were harassed by the post office in 1919. An Austrian immigrant, Berger developed a program of political action that, while operating under the name of socialism, was really a variety of moderate reform. Berger organized the socialists into a highly successful political organization by drawing on Milwaukee's large German population and active labor movement. For years, Berger published both a German and an English newspaper, distributing free editions to all Milwaukee homes on the eve of elections.[10]

Berger had won a seat in Congress, but was denied the seat for violating the federal Espionage Act. The government suspended mailing privileges for his English-language newspaper, the *Milwaukee Leader*. Berger ran again but lost the 1920 election. His conviction was overturned, and his mailing privileges were restored. In 1922, Berger ran for Congress and won. This time, the House allowed Berger to take his seat, and he served for three successive terms ("Berger long a dynamo of the socialists," 1929).

Although the German-language press in America during the Depression era tended to be optimistic about the new Germany, Hitler had his particular detractors in America. Many German Americans, still smarting from the experiences of World War I, preferred to be noncommittal. And, within the American communities, it was not all bad for the Germans. Though the Protestant Americans saw Germans playing cards, sitting in beer gardens, and enjoying Sunday frolics, German Americans had a reputation for being thrifty, honest, and industrious. From 1854 to 1856 German-language presses carried full accounts of battles against the Know-Nothings, informing the immigrant communities. The press reported the bloody riots and denounced mob attacks upon peaceful immigrants and their property. Some of the German-language newspapers raised money for the victims or provided them with competent lawyers in court. The newspapers also watched over the court system to verify that due process of law was observed.

Summary

The anti-sentiments of Americans toward many immigrants had roots mainly in economic downturns. When citizens of the United States lost jobs or were working hard but not realizing the American Dream, they often blamed it on people who had no rights and often did not have the language skills to defend themselves. E.C. Sandmeyer (1939), a historian, wrote about the motives for the anti-Chinese movement—economic, moral and religious, and social and political. Yet all of these can be applied to any of the immigrant groups. Whereas some workers were outraged over the immigrant being willing to work for less than the Americans, there were other Americans who believed their Protestant religion rejected immigrants who did not believe the same way. These religious Americans found fault with the Chinese religions, with the German tendency to enjoy the Sabbath at beer gardens and with singing societies, and with the Irish Catholics. Socially and politically, Americans viewed anyone who could not speak English as being not educated and therefore not in the same class as the American. This point was driven home in eliminating foreign languages used to teach schools and placing a strong emphasis on loyalty to the United States, as illustrated through the loyalty oaths pushed onto the Japanese. Politically, the opposition grew stronger when the United States was at war with some of the countries that had many immigrants in the United States, such as Germany and Japan. Politically, the Americans were fearful of the power that immigrants were learning to use through the election process, as illustrated with the Irish in Boston and New York. All in all, if the immigrants had known the level of persecution and anti-sentiments festering in the United States, they may have reconsidered their quest for the American Dream.

[1] *Newburyport Herald* (1801, June 19). Article retrieved from http://catalogue. mwa.org of Newsbank and the American Antiquarian Society.

[2] *Chinese American* (1883, February 3). Article retrieved from http://catalogue. mwa.org of Newsbank and the American Antiquarian Society.

[3] See Foreign Miner's License Registrar, 1860, 1862. State Controller's Records, California State Archives. Retrieved from http://web.me.com/joelarkin/Mon tereyDomographic History/Foreign_Miners.html

[4] *Irish World* (1874, January 3), p. 4. Retrieved from http://catalogue.mwa.org of Newsbank and the American Antiquarian Society.

[5] See http://www.loc.gov/exhibits/haventohome

[6] *Irish American* (1850, January 5), p. 2. Retrieved from http://catalogue.mwa. org of Newsbank and the American Antiquarian Society.

[7] *Irish World* (1873, November 22), p. 2. Retrieved from http://catalogue.mwa. org of Newsbank and the American Antiquarian Society.

[8] See *New York Times*, July 26, 1918. Retrieved from http://query.nytimes.com memarchive-free/pdf?_r=1&res+980DE1D6103BEE3ABC4E51DFB166838 3609EDE

[9] See trial coverage: http://query.nytimes.com/mem/archive-free/pdf?res=9A03 E1D91E3DE533A25753C1A9679D946195D6CF

[10] Available from http://www.wisbar.org/AM/Template.cfm?Section=Search& template=/CM/HTML Display.cfm&ContentID=35924

Chapter Three / Historical Context

With man, most of his misfortunes are occasioned by man.
Pliny the Elder (A.D. 23–A.D. 79)[1]

Migration to the "New World"

The argument is that *immigration created the concept of the American Dream*. As immigrant communities formed, patterns of development emerged. Development included newspapers—a deliberate creation of the community leadership—and through the press the dream was formed. Moreover, the evolution of the immigrant press has resulted in shaping the American Dream. The shaping begins in the past.

History of immigration to America starts with humans crossing the Bering Strait. The Vikings came, followed by the Europeans. As early as 1619, there were immigrants, slaves, indentured servants, and 50,000 convicts from British prisons. By 1790 the Spanish, British, Dutch, and Swedish were settling along the coast from New England to Florida. After independence, the United States became "an asylum for the persecuted lovers of civil and religious liberty from every part of Europe" (Paine, 1776). Between the years 1820 and 1880, there were nearly 10 million immigrants who came from the German Empire, Ireland, Britain, the Austro–Hungarian Empire, Canada, China, and Africa.[2]

The first Europeans paid their own travel expenses, but traveled in great discomfort. Many became ill or died before reaching America. The crossing was long, dangerous, and expensive. Shipping owners then figured out that once their ships deposited goods in European ports, the ships were empty. By filling the ships with people, the owners could make more money. As the need for labor emerged across the country and laws such as the contract law made it possible to emigrate, the number of people immigrating to America increased. The contract labor law authorized in 1864–1868 allowed employers to pay the passage and bind the services of prospective migrants (Briggs, 2001).

Between the years 1880 and 1930, more than 22 million people came from Italy, Austria, Hungary, Russia, Germany, Britain, Canada, Ireland, and Sweden. New modes of transportation, like steam-powered boats in the 1880s, enabled immigrants to come from the Middle East, the Mediterranean, and southern and eastern Europe. At this time, many people came from Norway, so many that in the 1880s, 9 percent of the country's total population had immigrated to America.[3] Before 1880, people arrived in America from any port. There was no processing and they were free to go anywhere they liked.

After 1880, two primary points of entry were the Angel Island Immigration Station in San Francisco, which processed immigrants from Asia, and Ellis Island in New York City. Ellis Island officially opened on January 1, 1892, and "the first immigrant to pass through Ellis was a 'rosy-cheeked Irish girl,' Annie Moore, age 15, from County Cork. She came with her two younger brothers to join their parents in New York City. On that first day, three large ships were waiting to land, and 700 immigrants passed through Ellis Island. In the first year, nearly 450,000 immigrants passed through the Island."[4]

Though World War I brought a decline in immigration, between 1915 and 1918, immigration spiked with the Industrial Revolution, which demanded a large labor market. Immigrants filled this labor need. As the railroads began to stretch across the country, people were needed to build the railroads, and then to create towns and establish farms to supply the railroads with food and goods. The California Gold Rush pulled people across America for quick money.

Economic advantage was one reason to emigrate. As sojourners, the immigrants wanted to make money and return home to reestablish their lives, but there were other dreams the immigrants came to America to pursue. As religious seekers, the immigrants wanted freedom to worship and not be forced to be part of state religions. As political exiles, immigrants avoided compulsory military drafts, civil wars, and political persecution—but wanted to keep their nationalistic feelings and ideologies. Other immigrants came to escape debt, or because famine, population growth, and landownership problems limited their abilities to grow and prosper. Each was seeking his or her own American Dream—a dream that was somewhat possible during strong economic times when the immigrants were abused but welcomed in the factories, mines, and railroads; but, if the economy was weak, Americans accused the newest immigrants of taking jobs.

Limitations on immigration began as early as 1882 when the U.S. Congress passed the first general immigration statute that imposed a head tax of 50 cents and excluded "idiots, lunatics, convicts, and persons likely to become a public charge" (Smith, 2003). Congress, at this time, also passed an act suspending all future immigration of Chinese laborers. The Supreme Court considered a challenge to the suspension and some subsequent changes in the Chinese Exclusion Cases.[5] Accusations against immigrants escalated during World War I with the rise of nationalism and suspicion against foreigners in America. The Immigration Quota Law in 1921 said that the number of any European nationality entering in a given year could not exceed 3 percent of foreign-born persons of that nationality who lived in the United States in 1910. For example, if there were 1,000 French citizens in the United States in 1909, then only 30 French immigrants could be allowed to enter. Nationality was to be determined by country of birth, and no more than 20 percent of the annual quota of any nationality could be received in any given month. Using the French example, no more than six French immigrants could enter during one month. If six came for five months, then no other French immigrant would be welcomed until the following year. The total number of immigrants admissible under the system was set at nearly 358,000, with numerous classes exempt. In 1924, a new Immigration Act changed the quota basis from the census of 1910 back to that of 1890 and reduced the annual quota to 164,000. This law ended mass immigration to America, started the process of examination and qualification of immigrants at the U.S. consulates located around the world, and changed the function of Ellis Island from that of an immigrant processing station to a center for the assembly, detention, and deportation of people who had entered the United States illegally or had violated the terms of admittance.

Who came to America depended on the push the immigrant got from his or her home country. Political refugees from Hungary often were intellectuals fleeing the racial and political policies of Nazi Germany. Hungary's political and social elite came to America after spending several years in refugee camps in

Germany. These Forty-Niners, as they were called, referring to
the war of 1949, were all political immigrants who came because
they lost their war of independence against Austria. They regarded their stay in America as only a temporary one that would
end with the liberation of their country. Based on the Displaced
Persons Acts of 1948 and 1950, more Hungarians came to America. The McCarran-Walter Act of 1952 and the Refugee Relief Act
of 1953 brought even more immigrants. The Fifty-Sixers or
Freedom Fighters were mostly young and well-educated males
who fled Hungary after the unsuccessful anti-Soviet Revolution
of 1956.

The Russian Jews also were pushed. Russia's May Laws, established in 1882 as temporary laws but which lasted 30 years,
severely restricted where Jews could live and work in Russia.
Jews were not allowed to live in rural areas or towns with less
than 10,000 people. They were also placed in strict quotas for
secondary and college education. As a result, more than three
million Russians immigrated to the United States. After the
Russian Revolution, the American government began to fear that
the United States was in danger of its own communist revolution
with so many Russians arriving, so the U.S. government tried to
limit political and labor organizations. Russian immigrants were
singled out as a particular danger, and their unions, political
parties, and social clubs were spied upon and raided by federal
agents. In New York City, in the 1900s, 5,000 Russian immigrants were arrested. Between 1919 and 1920, during the Red
Scare, thousands of Russians were deported without a formal
trial.

The 1930s and fear of a new world war brought more Russians to the United States. These immigrants were affluent and
well-educated, and many were able to find work in their old pro-
fessions. This immigrant wave also brought the latest intellectual and artistic currents from Europe. Americans were
introduced to composer Igor Stravinsky and choreographer
George Balanchine. By the end of World War II, more than
20,000 displaced persons reached the United States from Russia.
Embarrassed, the Soviet government began to enforce strict con-
trols to immigration in 1952. For two decades any Soviet citizen
who dared move to the United States became a nonperson,
stripped of their citizenship and cut off from contact with their

families. A thaw happened in the 1970s, and there were a number of defectors such as dancer Mikhail Baryshnikov, Nobel Prize–winning poet Joseph Brodsky, and novelist Alexander Solzhenitsyn, who had survived many years as a Soviet political prisoner. In the late 1980s, before the Soviet Union collapsed in 1990, hundreds of thousands of Russians came to the United States. These new immigrants were young and highly educated.

The Great Depression further limited immigration, and though immigration slowed, it did not stop. Between 1930 and 1965, nearly four million people came from Germany, Canada, Mexico, Britain, Italy, and the Caribbean (West Indies). After 1965, people came from Mexico, Philippines, Korea, Dominican Republic, India, Cuba, Vietnam, and Canada.

The Immigration and Naturalization Act of 1965 allowed more immigration, and as a result of the Cold War conflicts, immigrants poured into the United States. Within five years, the Asian immigration would more than quadruple with the surge in refugees from the Vietnam War. The U.S. policy changed during this period to give preference to professionals like doctors, nurses, scientists, and hi-tech specialists, often creating a brain drain in the home countries. As a result, in 1978, the U.S. government set an annual worldwide quota of 290,000 immigrants. This was raised in 1990 to 700,000. However, more than one million new immigrants still arrive in the United States each year, many of them undocumented. From the 1980s on, undocumented immigration has been a constant topic of political debate. The Refugee Act of 1980 instituted a system for admitting those who feared or had experienced persecution on the basis of race, religion, ethnicity, political opinion, or membership in a social group but not ones seeking to improve economically (Murrin et al., 2002). In 1986, amnesty was given to more than three million undocumented immigrants through the Immigration Reform and Control Act of 1987. In 2000, the foreign-born population of the United States was 9.5 percent of the total population. The number of undocumented immigrants is thought to be approximately 3.2 million with 300,000 arriving every year.

As illustrated above, people came to America from all corners of the world. They were peasants, skilled and unskilled workers, scholars, and professionals. Immigrants of all colors, shapes, and sizes were both pulled and pushed to make the journey. Pulling the immigrants over were the influences of family, friends, ministers, recruiters, and printed information about America. Some immigrants wanted to enjoy the freedom of religion. Others were simply restless and wanted adventure. They were lured by the possibilities waiting for them in America. Some immigrants desired economic betterment, and the attraction of land and opportunity pulled them to America. They had no land, no jobs; they were dying in poverty in their home countries. Other immigrants were pushed over when they needed to flee from personal adversity, career stagnation, or family disruption. Many were anxious about the future of their countries, which had been engaged in long civil wars or were hit by major agricultural disasters. Somewhere along their route, during the trek from before the 1790s to the middle of the 1900s, the notion of the American Dream developed.

The American Dream

America offered freedom to believe, to strive, and to achieve as each person thought best (Jillson, 2004). In "Letters from an American Farmer 1782," J. Hector St. John de Crevecoeur provided the first full articulation of the American Dream from the immigrant perspective. He "described and exemplified the dream that has beckoned the immigrant: get here any way you can, learn a skill or trade, study her ways, work hard, save, and America will make a place for you" (Jillson, 2004, p. 57). Thomas Jefferson, through the Declaration of Independence, offered a more articulated vision of the American Dream. "We hold these truths to be self-evident, that all men are created equal, that they are endowed by their Creator with certain unalienable rights that among these are Life, Liberty, and the pursuit of Happiness" (1776, para. 2).

In numerous writings about the American Dream was the notion that: "No one had to promise the poor of Europe that success in America was certain, just that it was possible" (Jillson, 2004, p. 126). This possibility, the promise of America, included "social mobility, universal education, free land, free government, free thought, and human dignity; economic plenty and industrial power—all these sometimes overarching elements were reconciled within one overarching edifice, that of the American nation, the United States. The various parts merged to form the promise of American life. It was a promise that offered the chance of fulfillment to men of diverse ambitions and diverse ideals" (Cullen, 2003, p. 191). In other words, it was the American Dream.

The dream actually began with the Puritan concept of the good life and the freedom to worship. The Declaration of Independence became the charter for the dream. Upward mobility was secured if one worked hard, with promises of equality, home ownership, educational attainment, and social advancement.

However, there are those who regard the American Dream to be a myth, unattainable for many (Herbert, 2005). Countless people worked hard, but were crushed by industrialization, overcrowded slums, and poverty. There have been others who were excluded: women, blacks, and Asians. Each wave of immigrants was exploited in labor, housing, education, and political representation. Then there were anti-Catholic movements, exclusion of the Chinese, and hostilities against the Irish, the Italians, the Puerto Ricans, and now the Latinos from Central America and Mexico. The Hungarian American newspaper *Szábadsag Naptár* in 1908 wrote:

> The past year holds extremely woeful memories for Hungarian Americans. Great is the number of those valiant Magyars who fell on the battlefield of labor, who were killed by the mine, were crushed by rocks, torn to pieces by machines, and burned to death by molten steel. How often the mail man brought the sad letter with the news that, in one place or another, Hungarians are being destroyed. The mournful list will have no end. Labor is taking its toll by the hundreds, and we stand before the burned and mutilated corpses terrified by the knowledge of our utter helplessness. (Puskás, 2000, p. 139)

Regardless, an American tradition developed and was maintained through stories and through the press. This American tradition was why people came to America to chase the illusive American Dream. Horatio Alger Jr., who wrote stories about the traditional American virtues, has become a synonym for the American Dream (Jillson, 2004). Alger wrote more than a hundred books with many of the titles indicating how a character in the story chased the American Dream. His stories included "Ragged Dick" or *Street Life in New York with the Bootblacks*

(1868), "Rough and Ready" or *Life Among the New York News-boys* (1869), "Rufus and Rose" or *The Fortunes of Rough and Ready* (1870), "Slow and Sure" or *From the Street to the Shop* (1872), *Sam's Chance and How He Improved It* (1876), *From Farm Boy to Senator: Being the History of the Boyhood and Manhood of Daniel Webster* (1882), "Struggling Upward" or *Luke Larkin's Luck* (1890), *A Debt of Honor: The Story of Gerald Lane's Success in the Far West* (1900), and "Robert Coverdale's Struggle" or *On the Wave of Success* (1910).

Just as Alger's stories were about individual immigrants who had dreams of upward mobility and success, each person who has come ashore to America has had an appetite for material wealth and achievement. Millions of people have come to America in search of a dream, an individual dream. They may have come as individuals, but arrived to find themselves labeled as a member of an ethnic group.

How Immigrants Established Identities

Ethnic identity is not innate in people. Membership in ethnic groups can be ascribed by birth, self-ascribed by kinship or choice, or pro-ascribed by others (Laguerre, 1998). Each individual who came often gravitated toward a pre-existing group and was labeled more by the people who had come before them than by who they thought they were. For example, Lebanese immigrants defined themselves in terms of their religion, village, or family before they would see themselves as "Syrian," as they were originally called by U.S. immigration through the mid-1940s or "Arab," as they are counted by the U.S. census (Beseck-er-Kassab, 1992).

Support for the membership within an ethnic identity is that there has been a discernable pattern of settlement among the immigrants. Many immigrants settled near others from their homeland. Similar language and culture helped the new immigrants to find jobs, housing, and food. Within these communities they first established a church, then social clubs, organizations, and finally newspapers. The newspapers were often in a language other than English with the exception of the British and Irish. Both the foreign-language presses and the ethnic organizations were viewed with suspicion by native-born Americans. What was necessary within the community, though, was the need to move away from an oral-based culture to a new culture, more dependent on media to inform members about religion, politics, home country news, and how to adjust to the new American culture (Hoerder & Harzig, 1987). In order to have a newspaper, the community had to be large enough and had to have a self-identity to support a newspaper. During the 19th century, it usually took at least 20 years of settlement before the group reached this stage of establishing a newspaper.

The newspaper became a link between the immigrant, the home country, and America, particularly for the first generation immigrants. They had strong home country language skills, weak English language skills, little education, and few economic resources; therefore, they faced much greater obstacles to assimilation than the second generation immigrants, who had had time to learn the American ways to succeed. First generation immigrants also seemed to have greater ethnic awareness than subsequent generations. And, within the ethnic groups, there were also tensions. The new people were unhappy with the existing problems of discrimination, exploitation, and exclusion on the part of some Americans toward the new immigrants. These new immigrants came with a nationalistic pride and a religious fervor that fueled American suspicions. To lessen this anxiety, immigrants formed liaisons with each other and established religious, educational, occupational, financial, and other such institutions to create a more Old World community, where the immigrants could function. Some of these liaisons and institutions that have helped form the immigrant community have been maintained by the ethnic press.

The ethnic press also supported religious institutions, which helped the immigrants to adjust culturally. The church would offer services in the home country language, offer an ethnic school for indoctrination of the young, and publish a newspaper in the home country language. These religious institutions also offered an informal network of ethnically enclosed cliques and friendship patterns. In the religious press, editorials frequently covered political topics. Priests and ministers were important sources of information for the immigrants. Due to the higher literacy and educational levels of the ministers and priests, they were more often the editors and writers of the religious newspapers. Church ties have been positively associated with news-paper use and particularly high for those who were active in church affairs, as history demonstrates.

Education also has been positively correlated to increased newspaper reading among ethnic groups. Asians, Jews, and Arabs have placed an extremely high premium on education for their children. Based on immigration policy in the 20th century, people with advanced skills and education were given priority to enter the United States. This has provided the United States with a vast elite immigrant pool, but this policy has also often depleted the brain power from developing countries. These elite immigrants read English and quickly assimilate into the American culture, turning to the English-language media for their news and information. Many occupational institutions require educated and skilled professionals. These professionals tend to be heavy users of serious media, seeking political and financial information to assist them in their careers. Through this process of advancement in the business world, immigrants who use mainstream media and work outside the ethnic community often are more aware of the perceptions that the larger, more domi-nant groups may have and thus are more aware of discrimina-tion. This awareness can lead the immigrants to desire more involvement in the ethnic community and can result in an in-creased use of ethnic media.

The immigrants' use of media is directly correlated to in-come. The higher the income, the more the immigrants seek in-formation in the media, whereas the lower income immigrants depend more on interpersonal relationships. This does not mean that the media is not used by the lower income immigrants; it does imply more of a trickle down of information or using com-munity leaders as opinion leaders to share the news with the lower income immigrants. The literary or belle-lettres press has appealed to this higher income and more educated immigrant population.

Media may provide relevant information to immigrants, but memberships in groups, such as the church and political or cul-tural organizations, also helped immigrants to adjust to a new culture. Immigrant communities developed clubs, benefit associ-ations, singing societies, and athletic organizations. Through these institutions, other immigrants, who were members, offered moral support as well as information that may affect the political socialization of the new immigrant members. This can be seen in much of the immigrant labor press of the late 1800s and early 1900s, where the voices of a few immigrants within these groups, who had strong convictions on particular issues, used these institutions and media to make their views appear to be that of the majority.

Leadership structures within an immigrant community imply that immigrants are more dependent upon their group leader than people fully assimilated into a culture. These immigrants often lack the most fundamental resources needed to participate in society and rely heavily on community leaders. Therefore, the availability of ethnic media or political information has been largely the result of efforts of a few active community leaders. Had these leaders not written or made available this material, a large part of the audience would only have access to the host media, which many of them could not understand.

Traditional gender roles of the home country are often continued and maintained after migration. Men controlled information published in the presses, as most of the immigrant editors and writers were men. This editorial role did change somewhat for women with the development of the labor press in the 1900s. There were sections within the newspapers for women and children, but these were few and limited. Women were active as co-editors of anarchist newspapers, but most likely were married to the editor.

The Immigrant Editor/Journalist

Within the immigrant community there were builders of the community. These people were usually journalists or priests, who became editors and journalists after immigrating and evolved into mediators between the immigrants and their new culture.

Editors immigrated to America for many reasons. Some came to espouse a political conviction. Some Russian, Finnish, and Irish editors came for a few years and then returned to their home countries to continue their fight. These sojourners had no intention of staying in America and had a political agenda to effect change within their home country. Some individual editors came with the idea that they would be able to make a living from newspapers. These editors and journalists found out quickly that they had to supplement their income by lecturing, writing pamphlets, or taking small organizational jobs in the labor and political left movements. Political left and trade-union presses had to resort to picnics and concerts to raise funds or had to get sponsors. As to profits, workers' publishing associations usually stipulated that any surplus income had to be used for the movements. Consequently, individuals owning a labor press could not usually make a living from it (Hoerder & Harzig, 1987).

These editors' contributions to the ethnic presses were a combination of their own convictions, both religious and political, and their personal journalism, which offered the communities much desired identities. By examining the information published by the ethnic presses, more can be learned about the immigrant experience. What was important to the immigrants, how they interpreted current events in the home country and America, and how they defined their role in their new home can be gleaned from what the press considered newsworthy and how the press presented the information to its readers (Potter, 1960). Significant contributions have been made both politically and culturally through the efforts of men and women who edited and wrote for ethnic newspapers.

The influence of the ethnic press in American history has been considerable. Evidence is offered through the experiences of three men—Abraham Lincoln, for using the ethnic press to further his own political goals; Carlo Barsotti, for using the ethnic press to fund his own nationalistic goals; and Joseph Pulitzer, for using the ethnic press to memorialize himself.

First, Abraham Lincoln in 1859 purchased a German paper, the *Illinois Staatsanzeiger* of Springfield (Wittke, 1957). The rationale offered for its purchase was to assist Lincoln in winning the election. The newspaper, along with other German papers, favored William H. Seward because of his scholarly achievements and for his opposition to nativism. Lincoln was considered a dark horse candidate, but understood the importance of the German vote. The *Illinois Staatsanzeiger* was in his hometown, and Lincoln bought the paper in May 1859 for $400 from Dr. Theodore Canisius. He paid Canisius to campaign for him in Illinois among the German voters. After the election, Lincoln sold the paper back to Canisius in December 1860. Canisius then was sent to Vienna as the American consul, where he wrote a biography of Lincoln (Wittke, 1957).

Second, Carlo Barsotti founded the Italian newspaper *Il Progresso Italo Americano* in New York in 1880; it was the city's largest circulation foreign-language daily newspaper. Barsotti wanted to elevate the standing of Italians. He conducted a major public relations campaign that established several New York monuments to recognize Italians. Among the monuments is Gaetano Russ's Christopher Columbus monument in Columbus Circle, unveiled in 1892 on the 400th anniversary of the Italian explorer's discovery of America. Barsotti also sponsored monuments to Giuseppe Garibaldi, Giovanni da Verazzano, and Dante Alighieri; all are located in New York City parks. He used his newspaper to raise funds by public subscription.[6]

Another immigrant who left his mark on journalism is perhaps better known for the term "yellow journalism" and the Pulitzer Prize: Joseph Pulitzer. He was born in Budapest and immigrated to the United States in 1864 to fight in the Civil War on the Union side. After the war he became a reporter on a St. Louis German-language daily newspaper, the *Westliche Post.* He bought the St. Louis German paper the *Staats-Zeuitung* in 1874, and then gained control of the *St. Louis Dispatch,* which he merged with the *Post.* The *Post-Dispatch* became the dominant evening newspaper in St. Louis. A scandal pushed Pulitzer to leave St. Louis and go to New York. In 1887, he founded the *Evening World* in New York City and turned the paper into the leading journalistic voice of the Democratic Party. He used publicity stunts, blatant self-advertising, and sensationalistic journalism in his newspapers. The competition with William Randolph Hearst's *New York Morning Journal* resulted in coining the term yellow journalism. Before he died, Pulitzer endowed the Columbia University School of Journalism and established the Pulitzer Prize, awarded annually for literature, drama, music, and journalism since 1917, and for editorial cartoonists since 1922.[7]

Summary

Immigrants were pushed or pulled to America in search of the illusive, not well-defined, but possible American Dream. Ethnic identity was established within the communities through the help of the ethnic newspapers. Immigrant editors and journalists, as community leaders, became strong influences within the ethnic communities and helped shape the experience of first generation immigrants to America.

[1] Pliny the Elder, Natural History found at http://penelope.uchicago.edu/Thayer E/Roman/Texts/pliny_the_Elder/home.html

[2] See www.ellisisland.com and http://www.olivetreegenealogy.com/ships/italian stousa.shtml

[3] See http://www.ellisisland.org/immexp/wseix_5_3.asp

[4] See http://www.ellisisland.org/genealogy/annie_moore.asp

[5] See Chae Chen Ping v. U.S. 130 US 581 (1889). This case is generally held up as the one that "finds" power under the Constitution for the federal government to exclude noncitizens as it sees fit for the preservation of the sovereign's independence, peace, and security.

[6] See http://columbus.vanderkrogt.net/us_ne/newyork1.html

[7] See www.newsscan.com

Chapter Four / Press Functions

We were born to unite with our fellow man,
and to join community with the human race.
Cicero (106 BCE–43 BCE)

Establishing Newspapers in Ethnic Communities

Newspapers serve a function within the community. This function changes when the community changes. Ethnic presses' functions have been defined by a demonstrated need to link dual cultures. Editors of ethnic presses added the functions of educator and advocator for immigrant rights. Some socialist and anarchist presses' goals were to agitate and organize. Many ethnic presses helped search for missing family. Along the path, the ethnic presses were forced to change functions in order to survive.

Historically, newspapers have become the public record of a community. Regardless of the language, or the group, or the association, newspapers have documented events of communities through the voices of their editors and the mission of the newspapers. If it was a community-based newspaper, then the news and information regarding the community would be reflected in the news. If it was a labor newspaper, then the news and information reflected problems of various labor groups and political viewpoints. If it was a religious newspaper, the information was based on the beliefs of the religious group publishing the newspaper. Like other types of newspapers, the ethnic presses had a viewpoint, and that viewpoint was strongly connected with the home country. In New York City between the late 1800s and the mid-1900s, no language group was so numerically insignificant that it did not maintain a printed press and publish some sort of periodical (Park, 1922).

Newspapers were the third stage of an immigrant community settlement after forming churches and associations. The newspaper was seen as a necessary part of the immigrant life as emphasized by a Polish journalist, Stanislaus Osada, who wrote "[t]hree forces were the main influence on the general progress and present status of the Polish immigrants in America: the clergy, the organizations, and the press. Because neither the clergy nor the organizations would be capable of accomplishing much on such a wide scale, the press is entitled to most credit" (Blejwas, 1993, p. 23).

These first newspapers were generally small weekly or monthly journals with a limited circulation. They had short life spans appealing to the immediate needs of the immigrants who read them. Once many of the immigrants assimilated into the American culture, the need for an ethnic newspaper diminished. Some of these newspapers lasted only a few weeks or a year or two. As the community grew, so did the newspaper. As the competition increased, the newspapers grew larger with the most successful growing into daily publications. The newspapers were important badges within the immigrant community because many of them were not permitted to publish newspapers back home in any language (Blejwas, 1993). In addition, the average person rarely mastered any language but the one he or she spoke. Therefore, if books and newspapers were printed in languages different from the one used every day, then the average person would not read and would have limited knowledge of what was happening in the world. As sociologist R.E. Park said, "When a man does not read, he can secure the ideas of other men only by word of mouth" (Park, 1922, p. 14).

Ethnic newspapers met this challenge of informing immigrants by publishing in the home country language. Many of these newspapers were closely modeled on the existing American press—from organization of the office, with an editor-in-chief and various section heads, to the structure of the contents into distinct departments. Eventually, many ethnic presses even created press bureaus and news associations. Other ethnic newspapers became the foreign language counterparts of the *New York Times, Boston Herald*, or the *Pittsburgh Post*, providing news of the day, sports, weather, entertainment, along with news of the home country.

Ownership of newspapers included the commercial ventures funded by affluent people with agendas, banks, and steamship agents, or the organizational ventures funded by associations, political parties, and publishing societies because a viable commercial press was difficult to achieve in the formation of the newspaper in the ethnic community. Therefore, newspapers were owned and edited by people who had the means to do so, like the clergy, more affluent people in the community, or people with a pecuniary interest in the immigrant community, like steamship agents or banks, or individuals with a point of view, like Yen Ngoe Do, who founded *Nguoi Viet Daily News* in 1978, a Vietnamese-language newspaper. The first copies were printed in Do's garage in Orange County, California, with $4,000 of his own savings. Today the newspaper has 60 employees with a circulation of 18,000.[1] Though Do's newspaper covers news, it has its political agenda. Most of the newspaper owners often had religious or political agendas for running the newspaper. Additionally, newspapers also were established to address grievances or for personal ambitions.

Some priests published newspapers when they did not want to educate the people or serve the church, but just wanted to satisfy their own personal ambitions and to support personal views and opinions (Park, 1922). Other newspapers were started for political campaigns and ended after the election. Racism prompted the development of some ethnic media. Other factors contributing to the development of media included conflicts with other ethnic groups or even among the ethnic group itself, sociocultural activism to promote the ethnic awareness, and community involvement of the ethnic media (Wilson & Gutiérrez, 1985).

Early ethnic newspapers were also owned by steamship agents and banks (Park, 1922). These publications were public relations tools to attract immigrants to travel to the New World. Political parties, fraternal organizations, and nationalistic movements also published newspapers for immigrants. These organizations communicated to new immigrant members with information that immigrants needed to assimilate properly into the culture, the area, and the organization. Another way a newspaper was formed was as a part of an association or club where the membership fee paid for the publication, and the newspaper was then distributed free to members of the association or club. A modern version of this system would be *National Geographic*, the *Smithsonian*, and any number of other memberships, like auto clubs. Within these membership organizations were labor newspapers, which were paid for through union fees. Some newspapers were cooperative ventures by publishing societies, where subscribers could buy stock. In all of these, the staff had to respond to the readership, and the editors were responsible to the board of directors. Though the society board of directors could hire and fire the editors and did exercise some editorial direction, their main role was to raise funds (Danky & Wiegand, 1998). An example of the reader–funded newspaper was the *Arbeiter-Zeitung*, a German-language anarchist newspaper in Chicago (1877–1931). As the first working-class newspaper in Chicago, editors were fired by the reader-owners when they disagreed with editorial policies (Bekken, 1995).

Each newspaper read by immigrants was also evaluated by them. These immigrants, regardless of their geographic background, often found English-language media to be biased, inadequate, and inaccurate (Viswanath & Arora, 2000). Therefore, the ethnic presses played an important role at many stages of an immigrant's adjustment to the new culture for believable information. The immigrants' evaluations of the presses helped to develop an attitude toward media and influenced immigrants' political socialization. For example, a Hungarian nationalist newspaper read by unskilled workers could rouse its readers to action but only when the action coincided with the needs of the immigrants. Therefore, the immigrants would be willing to support sick–benefit associations, entertainment, and churches but not trade unions where they did not have any members (Hoerder & Harzig, 1987).

How Scholars Define Ethnic Presses' Functions

Functions of the ethnic presses gain importance as movements of immigrants from one culture to another are examined. Adjustments had to be made within the American society as millions of immigrants from various countries, religious backgrounds, political indoctrinations, educational levels, financial resources, and skills came to America. These varieties created quite a challenge for the ethnic presses: How the ethnic presses could link immigrants to the American culture and still maintain the home country culture.

Ethnic presses linked the dual cultures of the immigrants by serving the following purposes (Joyce, 1976, p. 27):

o   Provided information about the new society from national politics to detailed legal advice on local and personal matters including naturalization processes

o   Kept contact with the home country by providing news
    about national politics as well as details about opportuni-
    ties for return
o   Provided information about the ethnic community and the
    transitional phase between the two cultures
o   Interpreted political, economic, social, and cultural devel-
    opments according to a particular viewpoint
o   Articulated interests of the ethnic group or a social sec-
    tion of it vis-à-vis the new and the old societies

Assimilation versus Acculturation

The first functions of ethnic presses included educating immigrants for their roles as American citizens, providing news and
information—particularly of their home countries, promoting political causes, such as nationalism, or defending the groups
against nativist attacks. These ethnic presses assisted the immigrants in forming their own identities. An example of this is
found in the Irish American press.

Oscar Handlin (1970) wrote in his well-known book *Boston's
Immigrants, 1790-1880: A Study in Acculturation* that newspapers were one of several tools used by Boston's various ethnic
groups to preserve their cultural heritage. The Irish used the
newspaper to develop strong cultural ties with Ireland and with
other Irish in America. The Irish could read the English-
language newspapers; however, they turned to the Irish press for
news of home, for accounts of Irish activities and organizations,
and above all, according to Handlin, "for sympathetic advice, de-
rived from their own ideas, on the strange issues they faced as
residents and citizens of a new world" (1970, p. 172).

This support within the ethnic community for their own
Irish ethnic group was maintained through the newspaper. Den-
nis Clark, in his book *Erin's Heirs: Irish Bonds of Community,*
affirmed the weight of the Irish press when he wrote:

> Their sense of community, strong in Ireland, had to be reestablished in
> the American setting, and that meant they had to adapt and extend their
> old traditions of oratory, verbal enjoyment, and political discourse and use
> the new inventions of newspapers, radio and other media to penetrate a
> new environment. While the Irish could stay abreast of American current
> events through the general press, they needed their own press to help

them share and shape their group heritage. The Irish American press
helped develop a coherent rhetoric of immigrant life, giving expression to
nationalist and ethnic goals. Irish-American journalism was a journalism
of controversies, with newspapers sometimes engaging in controversial
exchanges with powerful local leaders. (1991, p. 99)

Ethnic goals were cultivated through these early Irish newspapers by encouraging Irish Americans to form their own societies to foster both the Irish and the Catholic identities. The
nationalist press encouraged its readers to assimilate quickly into American society, but to also remember their responsibilities
to Ireland (McMahon, 1987).

The cultivation of community values is also seen in the critical role the German press played in German community formation, helping to arouse a sense of united Deutschtum (being
German) and reflecting and fomenting its divisions (Conzen,
1976). In the September 1844 issue of the *Wisconsin Banner*, the
editor stated that the press was a vehicle for consciously molding
German political opinion and must help form a sense of social as
well as political community (Conzen, 1976). The Polish-language
press in America served three purposes: to answer the desire and
need of unity and understanding among the immigrants cast on
a new land, to inform them of their duties and advantages of
their citizenship, and to keep them informed of the activities of
their fellow Poles in Europe and all over the world (Olszyk,
1940).

How Ethnic Presses Defined Functions

Examples of how ethnic newspapers functioned were gleaned
from editorial content. These editorials exemplified the functions
of linking dual cultures, explaining new national politics and
emphasizing home country information. Though many of the
newspapers provided these same functions, the purpose of the
ethnic presses was much more than just a means of teaching
immigrants how to assimilate into the American culture. Various
editors took on the job of being educators and advocators for immigrant rights. Many of the editors had specific issues they supported and wrote about heavily, for example, in the *Boston Pilot*
(1886), as editor, John Boyle O'Reilly saw his role to defend Catholicism against bigotry, to educate Protestant America about
Catholicism, and to bring Catholics, particularly Irish American

Catholics, into the mainstream of American society. Patrick Ford, editor of the *Irish World* (1883), urged his readers to seek vocational training, informed them of better employment opportunities, called for personal cleanliness and temperance, and cited examples of political treachery. Yuedishe Zeitung, editor of the *Jewish Times*, organized the Jewish Handworkers Union, helped new immigrants find work and housing, and sought to keep them from undue exploitation (Madison, 1976). The Scandinavian newspaper editors encouraged Americanization by urging the immigrant to use the English language and to attend public schools (Norton, 1977). The Lithuanian Catholic press interpreted the function of the press as a means to evangelize and to instruct the faith as well as the best means of clarifying the singular identity of their Lithuanian immigrants. These editors used the newspapers as tools for education and advocacy (Norton, 1977).

A function of the Chinese-language newspaper was to publish the withdrawals of members from a tong, one of the business societies to which most Chinese belonged. The tong required a person to place a public announcement in the newspaper. "Mr. Chen: I am a gardener and formerly of Ho Shin Tong. Now because I am too much occupied and unable to look after other things, therefore I hand in all the fees and withdraw from the tong. Hereafter anything that is connected with the tong has nothing to do with me" (Park, 1922, p. 127).

Along with these general press functions, the ethnic presses frequently targeted specific audiences within the immigrant communities. The socialist and anarchist press in Chicago had five audiences: immigrants, workers, trade unions, socialist party membership, and sympathizers (Nelson, 1992, p. 87). The immigrant audiences received news from the home country, often subdivided according to towns; news from Europe; daily market reports for foodstuffs such as bread, meat, potatoes, sugar, and coffee; railroad timetables; streetcar schedules; and locations of fire department call boxes. Advertisements for the immigrant reader featured steamship ads and railroad company ads for cheap western land. The worker audience of the newspapers received information mostly in the form of advertisements or announcements. Most advertisements were for food, clothing, doctors, housing, home furnishings, and entertainment. These stressed affordability and serviceability over fashion or extravagance. Letters from readers were published as were reports on fraternal and gymnastic societies. Announcements included births, marriages, and deaths (Nelson, 1992).

Trade unions were often associated with one newspaper. For example, the German furniture and metal workers and the German typographical unions claimed the newspaper *Vorbote* as their association newspaper. The Central Labor Union (CLU) included 11 of the largest unions in Chicago. The CLU's newspaper was the *Arbeiter-Zeitung* (Nelson, 1992). To cater to the German Socialist Party members, the newspapers explained socialist economics and anarchist politics to the readers. Lists of socialist books sold at reduced prices would be published in the newspaper. Additionally, there was often a Bulletin Board column that announced the time and place of party meetings and identified the lecturer and the subject. A short account of the lecture and discussion would be published later. Announcements would include election of officers, new members, and how the party was growing and developing (Nelson, 1992).

Finally, the newspaper would try to appeal to sympathizers of the socialist immigrant community. The articles published would chronicle the cultivation of the movement's culture such as the singing societies, theatre groups, dances, festivals, picnics, parades, and annual celebration of the Paris Commune, the first successful worker's revolution, from March 26 to May 30, 1871, which recruited new members and invigorated activists.

The fundamental tasks of the socialist and anarchist presses were to educate, agitate, and organize. By embracing class differences as the only alternative to assimilation and viewing conflict as inevitable, these presses offered articles that were provocative and inflammatory. In 1885, *Arbeiter-Zeitung* offered free weapons instruction, and the *Alarm,* the official newspaper of the Knights of Labor, advertised an armed section of the American group. The socialist and anarchist presses were influential during the Great Upheaval (Nelson, 1992). The Italian-language newspaper, *Cronaca Sovversiva,* listed addresses and relationships of businessmen, capitalist spies, strikebreakers, and other names who were enemies of the people. An advertisement published in the newspaper offered a manual for 25 cents titled "Health is in You!" as a must-have for any proletarian family. The manual was an explicit bomb-making manual (Avrich, 1991).

One unique function of the ethnic presses was to search for solutions and for missing friends. Abraham Cahan, in *Die Neie Zeit*, printed advice letters but expanded these to "The Gallery of Vanished Husbands" after the 1905 pogroms in Russia. The newspaper printed letters with photos, which inspired the United Hebrew Charities to establish the National Desertion Bureau (Madison, 1976). Every Irish American newspaper carried columns requesting information on immigrants disappearing into America (Mulcrone, 2003). This search for missing friends included 5,655 people sought between 1831 and 1856 through advertisements placed in the *Boston Pilot* (Harris & Jacobs, 1989). One advertisement was for Mary Burns Fitzpatrick who had fled to America with her lover. Her husband placed the following advertisement:

> Fifty dollars reward. Whereas a Woman, whose maiden name was Mary Burns, from Thorny Bridge, parish Porstown, co. Tipperary, Ireland, was upon the 31st day of January, 1842, married by the Rev. Mr. Hally, parish Priest of Gammonsfield, to one Patrick Fitzpatrick, and, in April, 1846, she left her lawful husband and came to America. She and one Bryan Laihy, blacksmith, supposed to be her first or second cousin, have since been living together as man and wife. She is now supposed to be in Worcester, or Farnumsville in Grafton, where she has a brother and two sisters. She is about five feet high, thin favored, black hair and very thin, light delicate complexion, with a small mole on the forehead. There are three spots of indelible ink in the form of a triangle upon one of her hands. She walks with a prompt and active gait. The above reward will be paid for her detection and apprehension. The much afflicted husband would feel obliged to the public by not employing her or giving her admittance. (Harris & Jacobs, 1989, p. ix)

Social services offered by newspapers included publicizing the requests of individuals and families in search of solutions. In the Lithuanian newspaper *Rytas,* a young widower unable to care for his little daughter pleads with readers to take her as one's own. Separated friends and relatives sought reunion. Or a disappointed bride-to-be craves justice as described in this appeal:

Augustas Bungorda, age 38, arranged banns of marriage at Waterbury with a widow, Anna Kulbokas, a woman with three children; he procured from her some gold rings, a gold watch and $100 cash and fled to parts unknown. He has a dark complexion, a hand marked by a bullet wound, and a scarred chin; he is of average build, has speech slightly defective from days in Lithuania...Let someone catch that evil one. The defrauded woman will give a $10 reward! (*Rytas*, 1896, p. 1)[2]

How the Ethnic Presses' Functions Changed

The ethnic presses' functions changed to meet the changes of the populations the newspapers served. A primary change in the population would occur when the immigrant community learned English. The ethnic presses then had to shift their focus. Instead of duplicating the English-language presses, the ethnic presses began to supplement the mainstream presses, providing information of interest to the immigrant community, information the English-language presses often ignored. The ethnic presses concentrated on news of the home country, on coverage of political issues of particular interest to the community—such as foreign policy and immigration policy debates, or naturalization procedures and citizenship. Since this information was less timely or pertinent, there was less information to print, and thus many of the ethnic presses serving English-speaking communities scaled back to weekly schedules.

Who was in charge also was a major consideration as to how the newspaper functioned. The editor was a major catalyst. Ethnic presses changed their functions based on the editor and the editor's prejudices. These prejudices had dramatic effects upon the contents of the newspapers. For example, when Patrick Ford was editor of the *Irish World*, coverage of Catholic concerns declined in the years of Ford's estrangement from the church. Coverage of nationalism in the *Boston Pilot* faded after John O'Reilly's death. Other ethnic newspapers began with one identity and had to change that identity based on the new wave of immigrants coming to shore. For example, the Irish American press developed first as a religious Catholic press and assumed an Irish identity. Even when publishing articles relating to Ireland and the concerns of the Irish immigrants, the early Irish American press did it from a predominantly Catholic framework. However, between 1847 and 1852, the Great Famine in Ireland sent approximately 1.5 million refugees to the United States. A press oriented toward serving an established, religious community was ill-suited to assist newly arrived, usually poor immigrants needing to know how to assimilate into American society. In addition, many of the new arrivals wanted a press that would chronicle and support the nationalist fight to free Ireland from English rule—the English rule that had, in the immigrant eyes, deliberately used the famine to drive them from their homes (McMahon, 1987). So the ethnic presses had to change.

Summary
Ethnic newspapers have played different roles in immigrant lives based on the stage of an immigrant's adjustment to the new American culture. The presses went from providing basic survivals information to interpreting political, economic, sociological, and cultural developments to mobilizing public opinion and unifying communities. The main function appeared to be in unifying communities. Newspapers established within communities unified the immigrants by maintaining language and culture.

[1] See www.nguoi-viet.com

[2] *Rytas* (1896), p. 1. Retrieved from http://catalog.mwa.org of Newsbank and the American Antiquarian Society.

Part II /
Missions and Motivations

Each newspaper had a targeted audience with a home country language. Though the newspapers fostered language, each had a specific mission for existing and were motivated by their editors as being a sojourner, religious, political, or literary press.

Chapter Five / Sojourner Mentality

How to Live.
A man should live in the world like a true citizen;
he may be allowed to have a preference to the particular quarter,
or square, or even alley in which he lives;
but he should have a generous sympathy for the welfare of the whole;
and if, his rambles through this great city, the world, he chances to meet a man
of a different habit, language, or complexion, from his own,
still he is his fellow creature, a short sojourner, in common with himself;
subject to the same wants, infirmities, and necessities;
and one who has a brother's claim on him for his charity, comfort and relief.
Norwich Courier (1831)

A sojourner is a person who stays in a place for a relatively brief period of time, often used in reference to tourists or short-term visitors or strangers to a country. Sojourners in America are people who temporarily emigrate for economic reasons, who want to practice their political rhetoric, are refugees, or who are employees or students.

The people who have followed the money generally have been interested in saving enough to go back home and help the family to start businesses or to build houses. Many send remittances home to families. Political sojourners have included activists, refugees, asylum seekers, and exiles. The political activists are the firebrand individuals who continue to fight to free their home countries from some political thought or action. Some of these activists have come to practice their political rhetoric and when it was safe for them, returned to continue the political fight back in their home country. Many of these activists have become editors or journalists, writing with great passion about the home country politics. Other political sojourners have been refugees who were fleeing violence, civil war, and death; they came for protection. These political sojourners can also be asylum seekers or people in exile, both seeking a safe place until they can return home. Modern day sojourners include employees of international organizations, guest workers, students, and diplomats. They come for a long visit but want to return to their home country after their work is finished. Examples of sojourners in the history of immigration and the ethnic presses include the Italians, Hungarians, and Chinese.

Follow the Money

Many people came to America with the dream that they would earn lots of money and then go home to a better life. Women from the Caribbean and Central America immigrated by themselves between the 1970s and 1990s; they contributed to the support of parents, children, and sometimes husbands at home. Some of them saved money to bring their families to the United States. Others returned home many times before they decided to settle permanently in the United States, much as the southern European immigrant men did between 1880 and 1924 (Jacoby, 2004).

Italian editors admitted that while their bodies were in America, their heads remained in Italy. These editors brought radical ideologies from Italy—varieties of anarchism, revolutionary socialism, and social democracy. Editors, often political refugees, included well-known propagandists such as Luigi Galleani, Arturo Giovannitti, and Carlo Tresca. American branches of suppressed Italian movements sent publications clandestinely to Italy. And, whereas, between 1900 and 1910, a recorded 2.1 million Italian immigrants came to the United States, at least 1.2 million returned to Italy (Danky & Wiegand, 1998).

Hungarian immigrants intended to use America as an economic springboard: make money there, return home rich(er), and make a life in the home country (Puskás, 1982). In 1880, ethnic Hungarians, as a majority, dominated politics in Hungary. The Hungarian government policy encouraged these poor peasants to leave and called the policy the American Action. Between 1880 and 1910, Hungarian migration was viewed by Americans as a source of cheap labor, and Hungarians viewed America as the Promised Land. The young men who came planned to spend only a few years and then return to Hungary with enough money to transform themselves into independent farmers or self-employed artisans. This is why they went into the coal mines and steel mills instead of agriculture. Only in heavy industry did they have a chance to earn enough money to be able to fulfill their goals back in Hungary (Várdy & Várdy, 1989).

Hungarians viewed their stay in America as temporary and made no secret of it. Many Hungarians made several round trips to Hungary. Between 1899 and 1913, 25 percent of the immigrants returned to Hungary. In 1908, the number of immigrants returning to Hungary almost equaled the number coming (96.3 percent returned) (Várdy & Várdy, 1989). Of the 2 million who left Hungary between 1849 and 1914, between 450,000 and 500,000 people returned to Hungary. Others who intended to return were prevented from doing so by World War I.

The Hungarians, numbering between 450,000 and 600,000 on the eve of World War I, lived scattered in nine mid-Atlantic and midwestern states and brought with them many of their ethnic and class conflicts. These tensions within the community can explain why no Hungarian lobby or central organization emerged. The communities were held together with the sick-benefit organizations, newspapers, and churches.

Returning to Hungary was foremost on their minds; Hungarians did not care about their image in America, and therefore were used often as strikebreakers by business owners. The result was that labor organizations refused to represent Hungarians who were forced to create their own sick-benefits and to handle issues of industrial accidents and deaths. These events were complicated with the language barrier.

Compounding their problems was a perception that Hungarians were not to be trusted. This was built on the fact that many never applied for, nor received, American citizenship but worked in the war industries at a time when the United States was not neutral. These Hungarian immigrants were thought to have been involved in sabotage. This, in turn, fuelled nativist sentiments against Hungarians, a group who was unwilling to Americanize, unwilling even to learn English. To counter these attacks was to publicly demonstrate Hungarian loyalty to the United States. An American-Hungarian Loyalty League was established under the auspices of the Committee on Public Information, President Wilson's wartime ministry of propaganda. This did not unite the Hungarian community, since the Hungarians had already established their sojourner mentality, but instead deepened the divisions within the Hungarian communities (Várdy, 1985).

Divisions within the community were not solved through newspapers either. The newspapers were divided into local, ethnocentric, and provincial between 1890 and 1950. A further division was along ideological lines; the newspapers fell into three groups: liberal-nationalist, socialist-internationalist, and religious (Catholicism and Calvinism). Three national newspapers were the Cleveland *Szabadság* (Liberty), New York *Amerikai Magyar Népszawa* (American Hungarian people's voice), and the New York *Elöre* (Forward). The first two newspapers were liberal-nationalist and the third one was a socialist-internationalist ideological newspaper. By the early 1920s, there were more than 70 Hungarian American newspapers in the categories of religious, fraternity, political-literary, and humor. Except for the fraternity papers, which were sponsored by associations, most of the publications were founded and maintained by a single person, who usually was the publisher, editor, and printer (Várdy, 1985).

The sojourner status of the Chinese also created problems for the immigrants but in a slightly different way. Racism had created discriminatory immigration laws targeted at the Chinese. The Chinese Exclusion Act from 1882 to 1943 reinforced the sojourner mentality by legally excluding the Chinese from participating in mainstream American economy and social life. These stiff immigration laws created isolated bachelors' societies in the mid-1800s. Most of the immigrants were male, illiterate, unskilled sojourners from rural villages in Guangdong. They kept to themselves and created small ethnic enclaves, which consisted of a small merchant class and a vast working class of sojourners whose lives were oriented toward an eventual return to China. This return was particularly important to survival of the Chinese community, since no Chinese woman was allowed to leave China without the captain of the ship giving a bond for her guaranteed return. This included merchants' wives and wives of American-born Chinese who were prohibited in the highly xenophobic, racist legislation after World War I. Chinese women did enter the country under special acts admitting war brides and refugees after World War II, but gender discrimination endured in immigration law and policy until 1965 (Zhou & Cai, 2002).

After 60 years of legal exclusion, the legal barrier to Chinese immigration was lifted post World War II. The enactment of the

1965 immigration legislation relaxed the immigration quotas with the stated purpose of encouraging unification of families and skilled labor migration. In the 1970s, the vibrant ethnic enclave economy of the Chinese communities encouraged a renewal of old ethnic enclaves and institutions and the establishment of new ones. The early Chinese communities did not include newspapers. Media was not important early on because of illiteracy, financial restraints, and interpersonal communication within the segregated enclaves (Zhou & Cai, 2002).

When newspapers did develop within the Chinese communities, the press pointed out racial discrimination against the Chinese and supported actions to fight racism. For example, the first Chinese-language newspaper, the *Golden Hills News*, published in 1851 by a missionary, attempted to reduce trauma faced by Chinese workers in the new land by offering solace and advice (Zhou & Cai, 2002). Advice included information on immigration laws and suggestions on how to deal with the injustices done to the Chinese immigrants by Americans.

Residents of California were alarmed at the increase in the number of Chinese immigrants. They were outraged that the Chinese were there for only money, ironically, as they were once upon a time. One of the newspapers, the *Farmer's Cabinet*, published that the governor was also alarmed at the increased number of Chinese immigrants, because it was believed that a large percentage of the "Chinese did not visit California with any purpose of continuing there" ("The Chinese in California," June 24, 1852, p. 2). Thus, it was an English-language newspaper that established the Chinese sojourner mentality. In a follow-up article a month later with the same title, the *Farmer's Cabinet* described the Chinese: "The hitherto locked up people are now daily arriving here in ship loads. They are stout, hale, hearty men, bearing every mark of intelligence. They present a queer appearance, as they walk in scores about the street in their native costume, with a braid of hair reaching almost to their feet" ("The Chinese in California," June 25, 1852, p. 1).

When the Chinese-language newspaper did emerge out of the community, its primary function was to report on mainland Chinese politics. Though the Chinese-language press served as a liaison between the different Chinese communities and promoted social activism such as equal rights and political participation, as did other ethnic newspapers, the Chinese-language newspapers also preserved Chinese culture by publishing literary and historical articles. The primary function, though, was politics.

Each Chinese-language newspaper in the United States was associated with a political movement funded by the Chinese in America. There were three political factions represented in America: Kuomintang (KMT), Youth China; Chee Kung Tong, Tai Tung Yat Po; and the Constitutionalist Party, Sai Gai Yat Po. The first dominant Chinese-language newspaper, *World Journal*, was affiliated with the KMT party. Tih-wu Wang was the publisher and described the functions of the newspaper in an editorial in the first issue of the newspaper: "To serve the interests of the Chinese community and to promote friendly relations between the people of the United States and of Nationalist China in Taiwan" (Lai, 1987, p. 27). Due to the rise in political awareness in China, nationalistic feelings and Chinese politics became prevailing themes in Chinese American newspapers until the end of World War II. After World War II, all of the Chinese party newspapers closed.

In the 21st century, the editorial focus, content selections, and programming of Chinese-language media outlets are influenced by place of origin and home country political affiliation. For example, the *Chinese Daily News* is politically pro-Taiwan, and "anti-communism" is one of its founding principles. In contrast, *China Press* is pro-China, and "promoting unification" is one of its founding principles (Zhou & Cai, 2002). The large and influential Chinese newspapers were the New York–based *Chinese Daily News* (also known as the *World Journal*), the U.S. edition of the Hong Kong based *Sing Tao Daily*, and the New York–based *China Press*. Together, these three newspapers had a circulation of more than 300,000 in the 1990s (Zhou & Cai, 2002). *Sing Tao Daily* is distributed in 100 cities around the world and maintains a news website.[1]

Though many Chinese languages and dialects exist, the majority of immigrants to the United States after 1970 were proficient in written Chinese. Once settled, they established new ethnic communities. These communities formed in the suburbs with strong economies and have been called ethnoburbs (Li, 2009). Economic development in the Chinese immigrant community is another driving force for the rise of Chinese-language media. The ethnic economy that developed from Chinatowns was oriented to sojourning and was confined to either ethnically specific niches, such as restaurants, or low-skilled, labor-intensive niches unattractive to native workers (Zhou, 2002). Businesses were closely intertwined with networks of co-ethnic members and their social organizations. Information was channeled through word of mouth and face-to-face interaction.

The survival and growth of the enclave economy depended heavily on ethnic resources—foreign capital, pooled family savings, ethnic labor force, ethnic consumers, and transnational markets. Chinese-language media has emerged in the immigrant community not simply as a service to ethnic businesses for marketing and advertisement, but also as a new type of ethnic business in itself (Zhou & Cai, 2002).

Political

Political refugees have come in large numbers to America. And, though the American immigration system and all its variants have caused the flow of immigrants to vary from decade to decade, political sojourners still come. These political sojourners include activists, refugees, asylum seekers, and exiles. At one time, Irish activists filled the editorial offices of newspapers, as did the Italians, Hungarians, Russians, and Poles.

The activists could not work in Ireland so they came to America and became journalists and editors. An example of the Irish committed to the nationalist cause was the *Irish World*. In 1876, the *Irish World* took over the administration of O'Donovan Ross's Skirmishing Fund to raise money to defeat the British (Rodechko, 1970). During the Land War in Ireland, Patrick Ford, editor of the *Irish World* in Boston, organized 2,500 branches of the Land League in the United States, and the newspaper administered a major fund supporting the Land League in Ireland. Support for the fight back in Ireland included keeping correspondents in Ireland and circulating copies there as well. On several occasions, the newspaper's nationalist ardor toward Ireland prompted British authorities to ban the newspaper from Ireland, which Ford did not seem to regard as any great disaster; indeed,

he almost seemed to accept it as a mark that his newspaper was
an important part of the nationalist movement:

> The New York daily papers of Sunday had a cable from London announc-
> ing that *The Irish World* of 23rd May had been "Proclaimed in Ire-
> land,"...They might as well have told us that Earl Spencer had breakfast
> on Saturday. The "forfeiting to the queen" of the *Irish World* has been a
> regular weekly performance for the past two or three years.[2]

Refugees

Refugees leave their homes in fear. International law, specifically the 1951 International Convention relating to the Status of
Refugees, 189 UNTS 137, has defined refugees and this definition has been adopted by American law and endures today in the
Immigration and Nationality Act. A refugee is any person who
has a well-founded fear of persecution because of race, religion,
nationality, membership in a particular social group, or political
opinions. Thus, the discourse in ethnic media reflects these com-
plications, seeking to address the needs of the refugees fleeing
political violence in addition to the other needs described above
(Sengupta, 2001).[3]

Refugees have come to America throughout history to seek
safety as a result of civil war in their countries, such as the
Hmong. Fifteen thousand Hmong refugees, the remnants of the
former CIA secret army of Laos, were allowed to enter the Unites
States in 2003. There are 180,000 Hmong in the United States,
with the greatest concentrations of Hmong in California and
Minnesota. The Hmong were offered refuge because they were
recruited by the United States in the 1960s to fight against the
communists in Laos. When the United States pulled out of Laos
and the communists took over in 1975, the Laotian government
allegedly sprayed lethal chemicals on Hmong communities.
Many escaped to Thailand, and now 15,000 have come to the
United States.

The Hmong culture has been slow to assimilate into American society and therefore the Hmong have relied more on public
assistance. The Hmong practice polygamy and traditionally have
treated women like property. In light of these barriers to assimilation, newspapers have been able to link the communities together and to discuss social issues affecting the community and
to advocate education as necessary to succeeding in America.

One newspaper, *Blong Yang* (Future Hmong), focuses on individual Hmong persons by regularly publishing a profile to show the importance of ordinary accomplishments for the community. The newspaper introduces new kinds of careers and nearly a third of the pages focuses on specific problems in the Hmong culture such as males valued over females, inter-racial marriage, pride/shame issues, and a culture where problems are not discussed in public. The newspaper is distributed free in various sites around Wisconsin and is written in English (80 percent) and Hmong (20 percent). Language is important to the Hmong. As a written language, Hmong had been lost as the Hmong people traveled through China and were forbidden to use their language. To save the language, the Hmong stitched the language into clothes to create tapestry stories, and then French missionaries brought back the language using Roman characters. Now the editors of Hmong newspapers believe the future of the newspapers is in English and want to give the Hmong people a voice. This voice is getting louder as every month the editorial offices of the Hmong newspapers receive more than 1,000 letters and even cassettes, catering to the illiterate and non-English speaking Hmong (Kenworthy, 2004).

Fear keeps refugee sojourners like the Hmong from returning to their home countries once the war is over. They fear that their persecutors are still free, or the traumatic events they experienced during the war make them reluctant to return, or they want to wait and see whether or not peace will last. Some have become accustomed to life in the United States and have children who are U.S. citizens. Others have relatives back home who are dependent on their remittances. Combinations of these reasons encourage the refugees to want to stay in the United States. Immigrants from North Korea and Cuba face even greater fears. Like the early Chinese immigrants, they will be imprisoned or executed upon their return if they left their countries unauthorized. Some refugees are forced to leave by their oppressors, such as refugees from Iraq. These refugees came to America as doctors, engineers, architects, and highly educated professionals. They then try to learn enough English to get jobs as dishwashers, maids, and janitors.

Modern

Modern day examples of sojourners include employees of international organizations, guest workers, students, entertainers, and diplomats. Traveling between societies inevitably involves some personal contact between culturally dissimilar individuals and exposure to unaccustomed physical and social manifestations. This can be unsettling, particularly if the transition is abrupt—it is the origin of the culture shock concept (Graham, 2004).

Individuals are more likely to seek out others with whom they share characteristics they regard as important and to locate media in their home language. These characteristics include values, religion, language, occupation, social class, nationality, and ethnicity. The greater the cultural distance separating people, the more difficulty they will have in establishing and maintaining harmonious relations. This has been true for most sojourners including tourists, students, and expatriate business persons, all of whom perform less effectively in their personal and professional lives in cultures that are significantly different from their own. Sojourners had to adjust to the host culture or suffer the consequences (Graham, 2004).

Sojourners often rely on memories to ground them as they embark on a new life in a foreign land. These memories serve as symbolic vehicles for ethnic identity for the first generation and for their children and grandchildren. Through memories, the immigrants and their families can remain connected not only with each other, but also with their home country, giving them a sense of always being able to go back, a way in which they can understand the motivations for emigrating and to comprehend the sacrifice. To help sustain the immigrants through the difficult early years is the notion that one can always go back home. Nostalgic memories also encompasses the desire for a place where one belonged, where one's racial ethnicity was not brought into question (Joshi, 1999).

A nostalgic memory helped a son and father connect with the home country. As they traveled back to Hungary, the father resisted. He did not want to go back. There were numerous travel difficulties along the way. Finally, when they did find his boyhood sites, many had been destroyed. There were no people who remembered anything about the family. The entire trip seemed to have been a big mistake, but then memories entered the conversation.

> The positive memories of his youth came back with my prodding, starting with that missing tree; those Gypsies; the artesian well with Roman inscriptions; the cherry, apple, and peach trees; and Liska, the family goat. And as we sat in an outdoor cafe, on a charming, curved, cobblestone street in Szentendre, listening to church bells chime in the distance, my father whisked away, with one sentence, the embarrassing comments, the lack of sleep, the hills he couldn't walk, his devastated Acacia Street, the guilt of surviving. He said: "I wouldn't trade this experience for anything I have." (Schreiber, 1996, p. 47)

These sojourners became immigrants who were totally removed from their traditional environment. They found themselves in new environments where no one knew them and where they knew no one. They had no prestige, no influence, and no moral presence, and though, as sojourners, they may have wanted to return to their home country, as immigrants they were freed from their past. Whereas they left behind not only their home country, their family, and their familiar circumstances, they also left behind their moral failings and questionable dealings. Past deeds were forgotten, their present situation overwhelmed them with uncertainty, and their future was dominated by a desire to be free from the insecurity of the immigrant existence (Várdy & Várdy, 1989). Many of these feelings and memories were enhanced by the ethnic presses. These newspapers keep the sojourners connected to the home country through news reports, stories, memories, and language.

Summary
Sojourners are people who believe they are in another country for a short amount of time. They are always looking over their shoulders to see when it would be possible for them to return to their home country. Sojourners stop being so when they begin to settle down, when they have families, buy houses, and create a life in America that they do not want to leave. These immigrants have shaped the American Dream around what they could accomplish or have built a foundation for their children to continue.

[1] See www.singtao.com.

[2] *Irish World* (1885, May 23), p. 4. Retrieved from http://catalog.mwa.org of Newsbank and the American Antiquarian Society.

[3] Refugees waiting to enter the United States have a medical review, a security check and an interview with an American official overseas. The annual quota for refugees coming into the United States has declined in the last decade. In 2001, the cap was 80,000; about 68,000 entered. In 2002, the U.S. State Department proposed a ceiling of 70,000. These refugees came from Africa, Soviet Union, and central and south Asia. A presidential directive is issued by the White House for the annual refugee quota.

Chapter Six /
Religious Intolerance

Religion stands on tiptoe in our land,
Readie to passe to the American Strand.
George Herbert (The Temple, 1633)[1]

Search for Religious Freedom

Immigrants searching for religious freedom in the "land of the free" found more intolerance than tolerance. These religious groups started newspapers as a way to maintain the religions of their home country. Many of the editors and publishers were priests and clergy. Clergymen were usually more educated than other immigrants, and they used newspapers to unite the community through the church. For example, the *Freeman's Journal* was owned by Bishop John Hughes of New York, but he sold it to James McMaster, whose aggressive Catholicism was a formative influence on Irish Americans during a critical stage of their adjustment in America. Even if the editor was not a clergyman, many of the ethnic newspapers published news as seen through a religious lens.

News was not limited to just the church when viewed through these religious lenses. There were other issues intertwined with religious issues that could not be separated. These issues are those of labor, education, and politics, and can be illustrated through the violence of the people who formed the Molly Maguires, through the struggles of the immigrant churches to establish language and church-based education, and through the anti-Catholic sentiment of the American Progressive Association and the Know-Nothing Party. In the end, the immigrants made a lasting contribution to America by giving the country its major religious strains: Protestant, Catholic, and Jewish. The religious press helped shape the American Dream, as immigrants came to America to escape religious intolerance.

Many variations to the Protestants came to America. As early as 1683, 13 families of German Mennonites arrived in Pennsylvania. Seeking religious freedom, they purchased 43,000 acres of land and founded Germantown, 6 miles north of Philadelphia. In 1731 Protestants were expelled from Salzburg, Austria, and founded Ebenezer, Georgia. Later, small German-speaking religious groups came. These included the Swiss Mennonites, Baptist Dunkers, Schwenkfelders, Moravians, Amish, and Waldensians. They came as redemptioners—immigrants who agreed to work in America for 4 to 7 years in exchange for free passage across the Atlantic.

Crossing the Atlantic was hazardous enough; however, the smallest ship known to have crossed with immigrants seeking religious freedom was the *Sloop Restaurasjonen*. This ship left Norway with 52 people and arrived in New York on July 5, 1825, with 53—a baby had been born during the 3-month journey. The Sloopers, as they were called in the many press stories covering their arrival, had come to America in search of a place to practice their religion without persecution (Rosdail, 1961). Influenced by British Quakers, they had founded new religious communities in Norway. The authorities in Norway did not approve of any religious direction other than Lutheran. The new Quakers were fined or imprisoned for conscientiously disobeying church law, refusing to pay tithes, and generally for resisting church-state authority.

The immigrants ran into additional problems once they arrived in New York. According to the 1819 Passenger Act, the sloop was in violation of carrying too many people and the immigrants were fined $3,150. When the ship and cargo were sold, the immigrants only got $400. This was to have been their investment fund in America. Since they were not aware of the law, President John Quincy Adams pardoned them on November 15, 1825. They settled in Orleans County, New York, and the settlement became the first Norwegian colony in America since Leif Ericson visited around the year 1000. Though the settlement did not last, the Sloopers' successful journey inspired "America Fever" in Norway. Hundreds of Norwegian immigrants pretended to be Quakers and came through this settlement to obtain material assistance and shelter. Once they were safely settled, they no longer had anything to do with the Quakers (Rosdail, 1961). In addition to the Norwegian Quakers, Lutherans came from Sweden, Norway, Denmark, Finland, England, and Germany. Each of these religious groups proved to have a variety of viewpoints. Therefore, the Missouri Synod of the Lutheran Church was founded in 1847 by German immigrants to combat what they saw as the liberalization of Lutheranism in America.

Wherever Scandinavians settled, Scandinavian-language newspapers began. Over the decades, more than 1,000 Swedish newspapers and more than 350 Finnish newspapers were founded. Some of the larger papers, such as the Norwegian *Decorah-Posten* (founded in 1874 in Iowa) and the Danish *Bien* ("Bee," founded in 1882 in Burbank, California), became national newspapers for their ethnic communities. *Decorah-Posten* was bought and merged with others as the *Western Viking*, which became the *Norwegian American Weekly* and continued as a bilingual publication. The publisher, Brynild Anundsen, a native of Skien, Norway, tried to avoid political and religious controversy because it had destroyed earlier newspapers (Lovoll, 1977). Churches also played a major role in preserving Scandinavian languages in the United States, as well as serving as important social institutions. Many of the Scandinavian-language newspapers were religious and were often sponsored or directly owned by Lutheran synods, the church councils. All Swedish papers up to 1866 were connected with a church (Hunter, 1960).

Catholics who came to America were from Poland, Italy, Slovenia, Lithuania, France, and Ireland. Clergy who edited Catholic newspapers felt the need to safeguard through institutional means the faith of the immigrant Catholics (Liptak, 1989). Both the *Catholic Miscellany of Charleston* (1822) and the *Boston Pilot* (1836) had long-lasting effects upon Catholic journalism and helped strengthen the faith of people whose Catholic traditions could be jeopardized by a hostile religious environment. Of all of these, the Irish especially identified themselves through being Catholic in a Protestant society. Catholicism had distinguished the Irish from their English (Protestant) overlords. During the time of the Penal Laws (first half of 18th century), when the government destroyed Catholic churches, imprisoned Catholic clergy, and confiscated Catholic lands and goods, adherence to the Catholic faith became, in and of itself, a form of rebellion. These strong ties to their faith were not forsaken when the Irish came to the United States. Indeed, the church was one of the reasons the Irish preferred to settle in urban neighborhoods instead of pushing on to the countryside. Rural America was predominantly Protestant. In the city, however, Irish Catholics could gather together, pool their resources, and establish a parish of their own.

This concentration of Catholics in the cities first became obvious with the arrival of the Irish. Prior to this, the American Catholic Church had been a small, mostly middle and upper class church centered in Maryland, originally a colonial haven for Catholics, and the coastal areas of the South, with some settlements of French Catholics in areas of New England (Cogley, 1972).

Irish newspapers also saw the news through a Catholic lens. The *Boston Pilot* tempered nationalism with religion (Mulcrone, 2003). Similar to the *Freeman's Journal* and the *American Celt*, the *Boston Pilot* emphasized the Catholic dimension of Irish American identity. Founded by Patrick Donohue in 1835, the *Boston Pilot* saw itself as an institution to protect the Irish Catholic interests in New England. Though it had no formal relationship with the Catholic Church, the newspaper saw the struggle between the British and the Irish as part of a larger religious drama (Mulcrone, 2003).

Other religious groups included Jews from Poland, Latvia, Lithuania, and Ukraine who migrated to America. The first Jewish congregation was in 1654 in New Amsterdam (New York); Sephardic Jews from Spain and Portugal arrived throughout the colonial period. Early in the 19th century, Jewish immigrants came from Germany. Jewish communities were being annihilated in Eastern Europe by a wave of state-sponsored murder and destruction. When the Russian czar, Alexander II, was assassinated in 1881, the crime was blamed on a Jewish conspiracy, and the government launched a series of state-sponsored massacres with hundreds of Jewish villages and neighborhoods burned by mobs and thousands of Jews slaughtered by Russian soldiers and peasants.

Between 1880 and 1924 an estimated three million Eastern European Jews came to America. The rate of return migration was close to zero—lower than any other major immigrant group. Unlike other immigrants who moved across the continent, the Eastern European Jews remained in New York City, choosing to stay close to neighbors from their old villages. The strict religious practices of Orthodox Judaism required that they live near an existing Jewish community. The community formed in America was in New York's Lower East Side, where they formed an ethnic barrier against prejudices. The Orthodox Jews had to overcome the prejudices of U.S. employers who would not hire the Jews for professional or industrial jobs. Orthodox Jews had to create niches for themselves, and did so by starting their own retail enterprises and working in factories.[2]

Controversies Surrounding Religion

Though people came for religious freedom, abundant controversies surrounded the various religions. Cultures were entwined with religions. They were so entwined that Patrick Ford, the editor of the *Irish World*, thought that political, economic, and social factors could not be separated from religion. Many other immigrant leaders agreed (Rodechko, 1970). The Swedes and Norwegians made no distinction between secular and religious items. Pastors were leaders in all aspects of public life (Norton, 1977). One particular Norwegian newspaper in Wisconsin, the *Emigraten,* was referred to as the clergymen's paper. Though the newspaper was political, it was published entirely by pastors (Norton, 1977).

One example of how religion was entwined with political, economic, and social factors would be the Molly Maguires. The Molly Maguires were an oath-bound secret society that resorted to violence, including assassination, in their fight against organized labor. Sixteen men were assassinated, most of them mine officials, and there were numerous acts of industrial sabotage (Kenny, 1995). In the end, 20 Irishmen were executed and 20 others were sentenced to long terms in prison. Though seen primarily as a labor issue, the Molly Maguires were also heavily influenced by religious tensions within the ethnic community. The Irish American communities in the western Pennsylvania anthracite coalfields were divided—half of the miners were Catholics from the western part of Ireland with entrenched culture, customs, and folk beliefs. The other half were Catholics from the anglicized eastern part of Ireland supported by the hierarchy in Rome, Dublin, and then Philadelphia. Both groups had a particular definition of what it meant to be Irish, and the differences resulted in a power struggle between rival groups and institutions. The major players, both locally and nationally, were politicians, saloon keepers, labor activists, a slowly emerging middle class, and the Catholic Church. Of these various forces and institutions, a specific Catholic definition of what it meant to be Irish emerged in the 1870s (Kenny, 1995).

Another example of how labor was entwined with religion would be the development of the Noble and Holy Order of the Knights of Labor in 1869, led by Terence Powderly, a second generation Irish Catholic. The Knights of Labor organization created a newspaper, *The Alarm*, which helped to develop one of the nation's most powerful unions, with more than 600,000 members, in 1886. The Knights of Labor was organized by nine tailors who proposed to organize both skilled and unskilled workers in the same union, including blacks and women. During the early years the members of the organization met in secret because members were often fired when it was discovered that they were associated with the Knights of Labor. To protect themselves, they developed ornate rituals, drawn from Freemasonry. By the 1880s, the group had emerged as a national force and had dropped its secrecy.

At the beginning, Irish Catholics shied away from the Knights of Labor based on their rejection by the Freemasonry. Catholic bishops also were wary of the Knights of Labor, as they comprised all labor unions. The bishops worried that many of the unions were cult-like with secret oaths and rituals. The bishops thought the members of the Knights of Labor might be susceptible to communist or radical influences, and that if Catholics and Protestants were mixed together, it would expose the former to the heresy of the latter. However, as the Knights of Labor grew in numbers and power, the Catholics flocked to it with an estimated one-half to two-thirds of the Knights of Labor being Catholic. With so many Catholic members, the Catholic Church was pressured to accept the union.

Other religious controversies involved education. Ethnic groups with their own churches wanted to combine academic studies and religious studies to educate their children. These schools taught in the home country language long before public school systems were mandated by state legislatures. The church leaders thought that language was important in communicating faith. They hoped to ward off any threat to the religion of their children by keeping the schools under church management. The Lutheran Church created German-language schools as well as teacher training colleges to educate the next generation of teachers to serve its private elementary and high schools. Most of the schools founded by new Scandinavian immigrants were operated by churches and other religious institutions.

These parochial schools where foreign-language instruction was used caused the American Party to adopt a program similar to the 1850s Know-Nothings. This program organized attacks on parochial non-English schools and lobbied for English-only legislation (Kloss, 1966). One such piece of legislation was the Bennett Law in Wisconsin, which required that church schools conduct lessons in English. The Bennett Law angered the German Lutherans in Wisconsin. The opposition to this law used the media extensively to promote its cause. German-language newspapers such as the *Herold, Seebote, Germania,* and the Democratic *Milwaukee Journal* were opposed to the law. The *Gemeindeblatt* newspaper responded to the governor's statement that Lutheran pastors and congregations had taken an oath "to darken the understanding of young people. This is false! Our leaders do all they can to give the best education possible" (Schroeder, 1976, p. 10). Although the Republican *Milwaukee Sentinel* came to the defense of the law, it was eventually repealed. The political success of the leaders of the German Wisconsin Lutheran opposition helped many of the pastors, teachers, and laymen obtain appointment to political posts.

Other laws attempting to limit parochial schools included the Edwards Law of 1889, which required that parochial and public schools in Illinois teach in English. The Faribault Plan in Minnesota was modeled on a similar plan in Poughkeepsie, New York, whereby the public school board would own the schools in which Catholics taught children. The only difference would be that religious instruction would be offered only before or after regular school hours.

Undaunted by the political controversy surrounding immigrant education, the ethnic press took on the issue of higher education. Ford, in the *Irish World,* cited statistics that showed those who possessed superior schooling enjoyed vast economic advantages over those who had left school prematurely. Professional training leading to careers in law, medicine, and journalism was considered especially praiseworthy for Irish Americans. From the standpoint of the Catholic liberals, higher education seemed directly related to the success or failure of the church in America. In 1887, the Catholic liberals specifically endeavored to create the Catholic University of America that would rival leading American and European schools (Rodechko, 1970). The Catholic University of America is the national university of the Catholic Church and the only higher education institution founded by the U.S. bishops. The university was established in 1887 in Washington, D.C. with the motto Deus Lux Mea Est (God Is My Light). The new university's faculty would become vitally involved in the church's encounter with American culture, particularly the social question of industrial conflict.

Other church-sponsored Scandinavian institutions of higher education in the United States were the Swedish Augustana College in North Dakota, the Norwegian Lutheran College in Iowa, and the Finnish Suomi College in Michigan. German Americans, however, did not realize their dream to have their own university with German as the language of instruction. This institution was to attract German-language students with different religious and political persuasions.

Politics could not be separated from religion either. Both the English-language press and the ethnic press discussed the differences in religions using politics as a foil. Rodechko cites the *New York Times* (1871, Feb. 2, p. 4): "charging that masses of Irish Catholic immigrants endangered Protestant security in New York and called for Protestants to rise against increased Catholic political power" (1970, p. 526). Ford tried to show that Protestants, rather than Catholics, were the unwanted intruders. In an article entitled "How Shall We Treat Immigrants" (*Irish World*, 1871 April 29, p. 4 cited in Rodechko, 1970, p. 526), Ford indicated that Protestants coming to predominantly Catholic areas of Brooklyn from New England possessed religious views that were "adverse to those of the original inhabitants..."(Rodechko, 1970, p. 526). He wrote that these immigrants had a godless manner of preaching, partaking of a theatrical character that allowed no respect for the more reverential and truer teachings of religion. The editor thought that Protestant services were not only "profane and demoralizing" when compared to the prevailing Catholic practices, but were "injurious to the morals of the young..." (Rodechko, 1970, p. 526).

The *Irish World* contained numerous articles that indicated that President William McKinley's policies were directed not only at generally backward areas, but also at areas with Catholic populations. Noting the intent of many Americans to have Protestant missionaries serve the imperialists in places like Puerto Rico, Cuba, and the Philippines, the newspaper cited supposed atrocities committed by American soldiers and officials against Catholic property and clergymen as indicative of the external or international expression of anti-Catholic sentiments.[3] To inform his immigrant readers, Ford published a variety of information about the Catholic societies, parish priests, and members of the hierarchy. Through his newspaper, Ford offered the final word on Catholic attitudes on courtship and marriage, divorce, suicide, and education. Within the pages of the *Irish World*, Ford discussed intricate theological issues and simplified these issues in an attempt to provide greater clarity and meaning for immigrant readers.[4]

Politics mixed with religion was also illustrated through the interviews and editorials following former President Theodore Roosevelt's visit to Rome in 1910. Roosevelt had accepted an invitation to call upon the Pope when visiting Rome. However, the invitation came with the stipulation that he would not visit any Protestant organization while he was in Rome. Roosevelt refused to abide by the stipulation and visited the Roman Methodists, who were mired in a controversy with the Vatican at the time. Roosevelt was then denied a papal interview. Ford was infuriated by Roosevelt's behavior. Ford wrote that Roosevelt must be a pro-British sympathizer and an imperialist, charges that the *Irish World* had avoided in the past.[5]

In an article published in the *Washington Post* on April 4, 1910, entitled "Clergy Lauds Stand," interviews with eight non-Catholic clergy supported Roosevelt's stand to visit the Methodists in Italy and not be granted an interview with the Pope. These eight clergy said that they thought Roosevelt had done the right thing by not allowing the Vatican to dictate who he could see or where he could go. These clergy were from the Presbyterian, Church of the Covenant, Methodist Episcopal, Unitarian, and Reformed churches.

One editor, who was enraged by some newspapers' defense of the Pope's conduct concerning Roosevelt's visit, was Thomas Watson, editor of the Georgia publication *Watson's Magazine.* Watson decided to expose what he saw as the Catholic plot against democracy.[6] Shortly thereafter, another editor, Wilbur Franklin Phelps, in the small town of Aurora, Missouri, published a newspaper called *The Menace* in 1911, which was also anti-Catholic. By the end of the first year, the publication had a circulation of 120,000. This increased to 500,000 by year two, and to 1 million by year three. Phelps also had a large publishing plant with 135 employees producing mail-order anti-Catholic books. The broad base of anti-Catholic hatred was in rural towns.

Religious conflict escalated into a huge anti-Catholic movement in the United States, which prompted the Roman Catholic Church to establish its first newspaper as early as 1809 (Baumgartner, 1931). By the 1820s, in response to growing anti-Catholic attacks, Catholics established other newspapers to defend their church and educate Americans about their religion. These newspapers proved more permanent than before and included such newspapers as New York's *Freeman's Journal* and the *Boston Pilot*, which grew into the preeminent Catholic newspapers in the country. During this period, some bishops, such as the Bishop of Cincinnati, began to publish the first diocesan newspapers (Baumgartner, 1931). After 1840, intensified anti-Catholicism, plus the necessity of reaching the growing population of new Catholic immigrants, encouraged increased support for a new expansion of the Catholic press (Baumgartner, 1931).

The anti-Catholic attacks grew more violent in the 1830s. Protestants burned down St. Mary's Catholic Church in New York City in 1831. A number of Catholic churches were burned throughout the Northeast, especially in New York, Philadelphia, and Boston. The most infamous incident happened in 1834 and involved the torching of an Ursuline convent in Charleston, Massachusetts, following wild and unsubstantiated rumors of dungeons and torture chambers. In 1844, anti-Catholic riots in Philadelphia left 13 dead. Warnings about Catholic political conspiracies escalated. The *Boston Pilot* (1854, July 4) carried reports of anti-Catholic violence—including bomb attacks on schools and churches—and concluded that a central goal of the movement was to drive the Irish out of the country by denying them employment. In response to the nativist attacks, the *Boston Pilot* emphasized Catholic identity even more strongly and mounted a counterattack against Protestants based on claims of the inherent moral superiority of Irish Catholics. In an editorial published in the *Boston Pilot*: "These papers hate the Irish and openly say so" (1854, Feb. 18, p. 5), and the newspaper attacked the papers that printed anti-Catholic articles such as the *Bee*, the *Commonwealth*, and the *New York Times* (Rodechko, 1970, p. 527).

The term "nativism" was coined in 1840 and developed over fear that influences from abroad would threaten the life of the nation from within. Foreign connections were seen to be un-American. Catholics were seen as a menace to American liberty because nativists thought that Catholics were sent to subvert American institutions. Stiff naturalization laws were established, and Catholics and foreigners were excluded from public office (Higham, 2002). Anti-Catholicism as a nativist theme originated in the Protestant hatred of Rome. It dates back to the beginning of the Reformation when the Protestant conception of popery was that of moral depravity, a conception which further developed into xenophobic feelings when all adherents to the Catholic Church were seen as dangerous foreign agents in the service of the Pope. In response to the nativists' attacks, the Catholic Church strengthened its press. "These journals today are of supreme importance, as was pointed out by Pius X, who said that in vain do we build churches and schools if we do not also build up a worthy Catholic press" (*Boston Pilot*, 1915, Jan. 9, p. 4).[7]

The Irish Catholics located in urban areas in the Northeast seemed to think that all anti-Catholic sentiments were directed at them. However, anti-Catholic sentiments were extended to all Catholics, including the Lithuanian Catholics, who were located in the Midwest and West. The Irish exacerbated this anti-Catholic sentiment by bringing the conflict between the Catholics and the Protestants with them from Ireland, as can be seen in this short statement by an Irish Catholic priest to a visitor in Ireland: "We have," said he, "scarcely such a thing as a Christian among us; Catholics and Protestants have only one common religion: that of hatred" (Pückler-Muskau & Austin, 1833, p. 407).

Many Catholic newspapers of the 1830s and 1840s saw themselves as active defenders and advocates of American Catholics. They were quick to take up Catholic causes and to respond to nativist attacks, though their pro-Catholic stridency only served to fan native bigotry. By the mid-1840s, the Catholic newspapers began to be more moderate (McMahon, 1987).

Anti-Catholic sentiments grew so large that the American Protective Association (APA) was specifically organized in 1891 to defend American institutions against supposed Catholic infiltration (Kinzer, 1964). The APA of Massachusetts, New York, the Midwest, and West directed hostility at immigrant American voters, workers, and officeholders. As a secret proscriptive society functioning until 1897, APA arranged lectures by ex-priests, distributed anti-Catholic literature, and opposed the election of Catholics to public offices (Kinzer, 1964). A Baptist minister of Boston, Rev. Justin D. Fulton, wrote books attacking the Catholics. He believed that the Pope had control over any and all Catholics through the priests and the members' faith. Fulton believed that Irish political victories meant Catholic domination. Other Protestant groups emerged to fight the "Catholic menace." The anti-Irish Catholic sentiment encouraged the British American Association to start its own publication, the *British-American Citizen,* and to grow its membership (Kinzer, 1964).

In 1892, the APA of Kansas City asked the newly elected governor of Iowa, William Stone, to blacklist all Catholics when making appointments. The governor replied, "Your association is undemocratic and un-American, and I am opposed to it. I haven't a drop of Know-Nothing blood in my veins" (Desmond, 1969). The superintendent of the Cincinnati Court House advertised for laborers and mechanics to work on a new building with preference given to American Protestants (Norton, 1977). In Boston a Committee of One Hundred flooded the press and the legislatures from 1888 to 1892 with anti-Catholic documents calculated to engender fear and distrust of the Catholics. One document bearing the signature of eight prelates of the Catholic Church called for the massacre of the Protestants on or about the feast of St. Ignatius in the year of our Lord 1893 (Desmond, 1969). Whether or not the document was fraudulent did not keep it out of the press, and the threat was published in *The Patriotic American,* a

Detroit weekly newspaper of the APA on April 8, 1893 (Desmond, 1969).

In 1893, the APA developed its own press and had 70 weeklies. All the newspapers had limited circulation with not more than 1,000 copies. Additionally, these newspapers were only printed around election times. The APA newspapers included the *True American* in St. Louis, *The American Idea* in Des Moines, Iowa, *The American* in Omaha, *The Loyal American* in Minneapolis, the *Rocky Mountain American* in Denver, *The Northwestern American* in Sioux City, Iowa, *The Allied American* in Cleveland, Ohio, and *The Patriotic American* in Detroit (Desmond, 1969). These newspapers were down to only three by 1900. Notices published in the *Rocky Mountain American* in October 1893 advocated voting only for Protestants: "Vote early and vote only for Protestants and in this way you will protect our free American institutions" (Desmond, 1969, p. 58). Tickets containing the names of the candidates with their religious beliefs were circulated before elections.

Again, the Catholic ethnic press was not to be ignored. They made strong assaults upon the new movement. Public meetings and anti-APA lectures and pamphlets were used. Council meetings of the APA were watched and lists of the members were procured and circulated. By 1884, membership in the APA was huge, claiming 2,500,000 members, including thousands of foreign-born people, the Anglo-Canadians, Germans, and Scandinavians—and even 20 members of the 54th Congress as members (1895–1897). Through size alone, the APA could have formed a political party but did not. The organization only captured Republican primaries and conventions and promoted local candidates.[8]

The APA was centered in the Midwest and fully exploited the climate of economic disaster and anti-Catholic feelings, blaming the economic collapse on the Catholics, "who had started a run on the banks in order to disrupt the economic system and thus prepare the way for Rome's seizure of power" (Higham, 2002, p. 82). The speakers of the APA organization told crowds of the unemployed that their jobs had gone to a flood of immigrants unloosened on America by papal agents. Labor was becoming more and more framed by the immigrant worker who sweated in the factories and mines. Native-born Americans began to fear the impact of the immigrants. When the economy was strong, Americans did not mind the immigrant labor pool; however, when the economy weakened, Americans were opposed to increased immigrant labor.

Besides the APA, anti-immigrant and anti-Catholic sentiments in the 1840s produced other nativist groups such as the American Party, which fought foreign influences, protested immigrant labor, and promoted traditional American ideals. American Party members earned the nickname the Know-Nothings, because their standard replies to questions about their procedures and activities was, "I know nothing about it." In the Questions for Admittance to the American Party (1854), inductees committed to "...elect to all office of Honor, Profit, or Trust, no one but native-born citizens of America, of this Country to the exclusion of all Foreigners, and to all Roman Catholics, whether they be of native or Foreign Birth, regardless of all party predilections whatever."[9]

The 1850s were particularly dangerous due to the rise of the Know-Nothing Party—which went after the Irish. John Mitchel, in his newspaper the *Irish Citizen* in New York, published an account of the situation in Maine. He described the growth of the Know-Nothing sentiment:

> February 1854—It was in these early months of 1854 that the native American mind began to take genuine alarm about the "foreign vote," and the Pope of Rome, and the Jesuits, and the perilous influx of "ignorant foreigners." They thought, naturally, that their institutions (which require, as we know, high cultivation for their proper use and development) would be corrupted and destroyed by this unlimited influx of illiterate outsiders, especially Papists; persons who had not been educated in our common schools. (Mitchel, 1876/1997, p. 363)

The *New York Weekly Register*, founded in 1833 and edited by Rev. Joseph Schneller, put special emphasis on Irish news and the defense of Irish immigrants from attack by nativists (Joyce, 1976). In addition, the *Catholic Intelligencer—The Jesuit*, managed for Bishop Fenwick by the Roman Catholic Auxiliary Society, extended most of its effort protesting restraints on Catholic freedom and discrimination against Catholics in Massachusetts (Foik, 1930/1969). The Scandinavian religious press carefully explained the Know-Nothing movement to their readers—then rejected it. The movement was found to be anti-immigrant, anti-Catholic, and anti-American, while hypocritically masquerading as pro-American (Norton, 1977).

Religious intolerance was seen early on to be un-American. The first settlers came for religious freedom. Many, however, found religious intolerance instead. A bright moment, though, can be found with the Plain People's newspaper, the *Budget*. A small community weekly for the people of Sugarcreek, Ohio, the newspaper had a national edition with a circulation of 20,000 and a local circulation of 10,000 in 2009. The newspaper prints news letters from correspondents, Plain People, who are the Amish of the old order Mennonites and similar faithful throughout the world. The newspaper began on May 15, 1890, by John C. Miller, an Amish Mennonite known as Budget John. The news items include letters from correspondents writing about the weather, crops, livestock sales, farm accidents, construction work, visiting and traveling as well as preaching services, illness, and weddings. The newspaper accepts commercial advertisements along with notices of public auctions, sales, showers, and related social or business events. Included are columns on Plain People history and cooking, as well as an information exchange. By 1990, the *Budget* was receiving about 300 letters a week and could only publish half of them.

One letter from an English person from Iowa explained why she enjoyed reading the newspaper:

> It lifted my spirits tremendously to know that somewhere in this crazy, mixed-up world there are people who care about something besides money, fancy cars, and $100,000 houses. They care about people! Their friends and neighbors and even those whom they don't know too well. And that's where it's at—that's what living and loving life is all about. (Guillory, 1985, p. 9)

Summary

The ethnic religious press has grown from one that was defending its religious principles to one with worldwide circulation. Through the history of religious ethnic presses, all news was viewed through the religious lens. Religious editors used the press to preserve the ideals of the church, to preach their own views, and to defend the church. With home far away, religion was a unifying structure for the immigrants, who devoured and believed the information published in the religious newspapers. Controversies in society were strongest against the Catholics, which gave justification for the Catholic ethnic press to publish the Catholic point of view.

[1] *The Temple* collection of Herbert's work was published by Wall, J. N. (1981). *George Herbert: The Country Parson and the Temple*. Mahwah, NJ: Paulist Press, Inc.

[2] See "Immigration, Polish/Russian, a People at Risk." Retrieved from http://memory.lo9c.gov/learn/features/i,,ig/alt/polish5.html.

[3] Published in several issues of the *Irish World*, January 6, 1900, p. 5; February 3, 1900, p. 4; February 10, 1900, p. 13; May 31, 1902, p. 4; January 17, 1903, p. 4; and January 24, 1903, pp. 1 & 4, Retrieved from http://catalog.mwa.org of Newsbank and the American Antiquarian Society.

[4] Published in several issues of the *Irish World,* February 1, 1873, p. 3; May 17, 1873, p. 4; January 3, 1874, p. 7; February 14, 1874, p. 7; and February 28, 1874, p. 5, Retrieved from http://catalog.mwa.org of Newsbank and the American Antiquarian Society; and Rodechko, p. 527.

[5] Published in several issues of the *Irish World*, May 28, 1910, p. 4; April 30, 1910, p. 4; June 11, 1910, p. 4, Retrieved from http://catalog.mwa.org of Newsbank and the American Antiquarian Society.

[6] See Woodward, C. V. (1938). *Tom Watson*. New York: MacMillan.

[7] Retrieved from http://catalog.mwa.org of Newsbank and the American Antiquarian Society.

[8] See The American Protective Association http://www.newadvent.org/cathen 01426a.htm.

[9] See Library of Congress, Immigration, available from http://memory.loc.gov mssmcc/062/0001.jpg and http://ctah.binghamton.edu/student/anderson/an derson4.html.

Chapter Seven /
Political Press Issues

A good newspaper, I suppose, is a Nation talking to itself.
Arthur Miller (1961)[1]

Politics is defined by *Merriam-Webster's Collegiate Dictionary* as the total complex of relations between people living in a society and/or the relations or conduct in a particular area of experience, especially as seen or dealt with from a political point of view. If politics was one reason immigrants left their home countries to come to America, then politics was also a way they defined themselves in the new society, often seeing their life work from a political point of view. Political persecution was not limited to just the home country America formed its own set of persecution methods.

Politics of the new America involved many immigrant issues. At first, immigrants had tremendous nationalistic pride for their home country. This nationalistic advocacy changed into advocacy for labor issues when the immigrants realized that they would not go home again. Through the ethnic press the immigrants began to shape the American Dream into a life that was tolerable through labor reform. Both elements of the political press—nationalistic and labor reform—brought their own tensions.

Nationalistic ethnic presses would transfer the tensions in the home countries to America. As immigrants became involved in American politics and more and more foreign-born people were elected to public office, tensions developed within the established political parties regarding the immigrants. Ethnic press editors spoke out against some of the American policies, especially those dealing with the immigrants' home countries, immigration, or a war involving America, but seen differently by the immigrants. Various ethnic presses were involved in propaganda scandals during war times.

The immigrant population helped form many of the early American institutions, political formations, labor structures, and social issues. Nationalistic spirits of the immigrants set them apart from native-born Americans regardless of why they came to America: to chase their version of the American Dream or to

escape political persecution, or even how they came as redemptioners, contract labor, through the padrone system, or with their
own money. Ethnic presses got involved in politics with heated
debates in the presses on labor issues such as the 8-hour day,
fines against workers, safety laws, a minimum working wage, a
40-hour workweek, employer policies, governmental intervention, technological changes, hiring practices, housing reform, and
land reform. By fighting for each of these issues, the ethnic press
helped shape the American Dream from a vision of utopia to one
of reality with the understanding that there needed to be a fight
for changes to make life even tolerable for many.

The Nationalist Ethnic Press

One function of the ethnic press was to link the immigrants
in America with the home country; newspapers performed this
function quite well. Many of the ethnic newspapers emphasized
the news from the home country. Others used the newspapers as
a soapbox to continue the rhetoric, loud and controversial, of issues from the home country. To keep these issues alive in the
American immigrant communities, ethnic presses supported political causes in the home country to include the Germans, Chinese, Lithuanians, Sicilians, Norwegian, Danish, and Irish.
These newspaper editors and publishers had every intention of
returning home to continue the fight; therefore, many smuggled
copies of their newspapers into the home country to strengthen
their fight and to secure their freedom.

The German Forty-Eighters, a revolutionary group, came to
America as refugees and founded the Marxist movement in
America in 1848. They brought with them what Americans considered to be unorthodox ideas (Higham, 2002). One of these Forty-Eighters was a Polish-born political refugee, Frederick
Fratney, who fled Austria and came to the United States. He began editing a German newspaper, *Volksfreund,* in Milwaukee.
His unorthodox ideas included free speech, trial by jury, and representative forms of government. Fratney preached independence of thought and the need for education. Through his
newspaper, it was obvious that he hated Catholics and the Irish.
Ironically, his wife was an Irish Catholic. Fratney Street in Milwaukee was named for him in 1857, two years after his death.
This revolutionary German press in America also supported vi-

olence. During the Chicago Haymarket Affair, German-language newspapers instructed readers on how to manufacture dynamite (David, 1963).

Though the Germans introduced radical ideas to Americans, the Chinese kept to themselves and organized their American communities politically, as they would in China. Chinese immigrants were united under an umbrella group called the Hui-Kuan or the Chinese Consolidated Benevolent Associations, referred to simply as the Chinese Six Companies. By the 1890s, 95 percent of the Chinese in the United States belonged to one of these regional associations. The Chinese-language press in America called this Six Companies' system the Kapitan China system or Shen-shang, meaning gentry merchant, because the associations were all headed by imported notables (Lee, 1988).

Just as the Germans and Chinese brought their politics with them, so did the Lithuanians. All Lithuanian publications had been suppressed in Russia from 1864 to 1904. So when Jonas Šliūpas began editing the *Lietuwiszkasis Balsas* (Lithuanian Voice) in New York from July 1885 to February 1889, he was able to obtain articles from many important Lithuanian authors. His paper was political, a champion of Lithuanian national rights, and a militant opponent of Russian oppression. The newspaper was smuggled into Lithuania (Balys, 1976).

Nationalist fighting also continued with Sicilian artisans and peasants as they arrived in America. *L'Adunata Dei Refrattari* (The Call of the Refractaires) was published in New York from 1922 to 1971. This newspaper was an anarchist paper with political comments on international situations. In 1944–1945, three issues of the newspaper were secretly introduced into Italy (Hoerder & Harzig, 1987).

Another party newspaper published in America and introduced into the mother country was the *Hindustan Ghadar*, founded in San Francisco by Indian immigrants. The early issues in 1912 were handwritten and the staff memorized a thousand names of subscribers so that no evidence could fall into the hands of the British government. Copies of the newspaper were hand carried to India and were banned by the British Indian government.[2]

Norwegian nationalists published the *Arbeidets Ridder* newspaper in Minneapolis. This was a publication of the Scandinavian Labor and Sick Benefit Society that supported workers' reforms. Labor and party organizational news was mentioned in the local news columns; however, news from Norway was emphasized.

Den Danske Pioneer (The Danish Pioneer), still being published in Chicago from 1880, was confiscated and forbidden in Denmark in the 1880s and 1890s, as the editor was critical of Danish politics during the Estrup regime. The editor, Sophus Neble, was a printer and a dairy-worker—not a socialist. His wife and co-editor was the daughter of one of the leaders of the Danish labor movement and active in the Danish American radical circles. The efforts of the Nebles, through their newspaper, resulted in collecting a large amount of money from Danish American workers to support the Danish labor movement in Norway during the great 1899 Norwegian labor lockout. The amount of money the newspaper collected was larger than that collected from people living in Norway and Sweden. Neble's political participation in Danish politics through his newspaper enabled him to be invited to Denmark as a guest of the Danish labor movement (Nelson, 2006). Years later Denmark supported the newspaper by commemorating its 100th anniversary with Queen Margrethe II knighting Poul Andersen, the editor, in 1982 for his work to unite the Danish American community. The queen returned to knight the next editor, Chris Steffenson, on the newspaper's 125th anniversary in 1987.[3] Obviously the nationalist press won the Danish government's respect.

The Irish press in America did not have British respect. The editors of the newspapers were leaders of the failed Young Ireland's attempted rebellion in 1848. These leaders sought safe exile in America. The leaders continued their efforts to educate the Irish people in America to prepare for revolution through several nationalist newspapers. These leader exiles provided the core of trained writers and editors needed to start a new wave of Irish papers. Their argument was that the church and its opposition to the movement and its support for the English government was the reason the movement failed. The rise of the Fenians in the 1860s only fueled this antagonism as nationalists enthusiastically supported the Fenian Rising and the Catholic Church condemned the Fenians as a secret, oath-bound society, which no Catholic could purportedly join in good conscience. The Irish newspaper, *America*, though published by the Jesuits, found grounds for supporting armed rebellion (Joyce, 1976). The newspapers the *Irish Nation* and *Gaelic American* paid little attention to anything happening in America; their full attention was focused on the struggle in Ireland.

Immigrant Editors/Illustrators Involved in Politics

Thomas D'Arcy McGee fled Ireland disguised as a priest. He was a member of the Young Irelanders. He began *The Nation* on October 28, 1848, in New York. His primary interest was the liberation of Ireland. Bishop John Hughes of New York wrote an article for the New York *Freeman's Journal* criticizing the Young Irelanders. McGee responded with an accusation that the Irish clergy was responsible for the collapse of the Irish revolution, that the clergy had not stood up in support of the lay leaders, and had forced the Irish people to not resist the British. The fight was on and the two men went back and forth in their respective newspapers blasting each other. Political pressure and a declining circulation encouraged McGee to leave New York. He decided that he would return to Ireland and fight the battle there. Friends, however, reminded him that if he returned to Ireland he would be arrested, so he went to Boston, where he edited *The Celt*, maintaining the nationalist fervor he had had when editing *The Nation* (Joyce, 1976).

Nationalism for Ireland was a major part of many of the Irish presses in America. O'Donovan Rossa, using his newspaper the *United Irishman*, solicited money to do as much damage to Great Britain as possible. Rossa wrote in his newspaper that the funds could be used to pay for terrorist-type acts that would make England grant freedom to Ireland (Joyce, 1976).

Freedom from England dominated Irish newspapers in America as Irish nationalists were exiled. John Boyle O'Reilly had served in the British Army and joined the Fenians while in the army. He was arrested for recruiting fellow Irish officers into the Fenians. British courts sentenced him to a penal colony in Western Australia from where he escaped after a couple of years and made his way to Philadelphia in 1869. Once in America, he became involved with the American wing of the Fenians and supported himself as a journalist. Patrick Donahoe hired O'Reilly as a reporter for the *Boston Pilot* in 1870 and sent him to cover the 1870 Fenian invasion of Canada. O'Reilly was made editor of the paper from 1876 to 1890. Disillusioned with the Fenians' inefficiency and internal feuding, he severed ties, though he remained close with other ex-Fenian leaders in the United States and remained a nationalist. He was a highly sought speaker and organizer for nationalist meetings, conventions, and rallies and donated considerable time and money to the nationalist cause. As a Catholic layman and editor, he supported Catholic colonization of the West and helped to organize the founding of the Catholic University of America (McManamin, 1976).

Another immigrant who took up pen and tackled politics was Thomas Nast, who was born on September 27, 1840, in Landau, Germany. He migrated to America with his mother and sister in 1846 with his father following four years later. He hated school, did poorly and eventually left, never learning to read or write. He had difficulty speaking English. He did attend an art school as he loved to draw. Through persistence, he got an assignment from Frank Leslie, publisher of *Frank Leslie's Illustrated Newspaper,* to draw a picture of the crowd boarding the ferry. He was hired. He later worked for *Harper's Weekly* and the *New York Illustrated News* (Paine, 1904). When the Civil War broke out in America in 1861, Nast covered the war as an illustrator for *Harper's Weekly.* "Thomas Nast has been our best recruiting sergeant," said Abraham Lincoln near the close of the Civil War. "His emblematic cartoons have never failed to arouse enthusiasm and patriotism, and have always seemed to come just when these articles were getting scarce" (Paine, 1904, p. 69).

In 1862, he drew his first Christmas drawings for *Harper's Weekly*. Not being able to read, he had his wife read to him while he drew. One night she read Clement Moore's poem *'Twas a Night Before Christmas.* This story became Nast's inspiration for Santa. He was the first to establish that Santa's home was in the North Pole. In this way, Santa did not belong to any one country—he became a citizen of the world. Nast also created Santa having a workshop with elves, established that bad children did not receive gifts, expanded the custom of sending a letter to Santa, and though the custom of kissing under the mistletoe was known in Europe, Nast brought the custom to America through his drawings. It was also Nast's drawings of Santa that inspired the American government to establish Christmas Day as December 25 in all states and territories in the United States (Paine, 1904).

Nast's influence on American politics only grew through his cartoons and engravings. He created the concept of the Republican elephant and Democratic donkey. He also contributed to how Uncle Sam looks today (Paine, 1904).

Politics in America

The ethnic press also was involved in American politics. The desire to protect all things related to the immigrant experience was too strong to limit the ethnic press to the home country and to the issues within the ethnic communities. The editors of the newspapers got involved in American politics. Examples include the Polish and Irish presses. The Polish press believed in a free Poland. They came to fight (Hunter, 1960). Fighting also meant finding ways to fight, like working through the established political systems—specifically, getting elected to office. One Polish editor, Louis Hammerling, received subsidies to support the Republican Party. He made arrangements with Senators Mark Hanna and Boises Penrose that he would influence ethnic newspapers in favor of Republican candidates in exchange for a subsidy (Park, 1922). Hammerling organized the ethnic newspapers under the American Association of Foreign Language Newspapers. Hammerling kept the association's member newspapers loyal to the Republican Party in return for corporate advertising. At the same time, he also tried to keep the Republican leaders loyal to the immigrants. With 508 newspapers in the association, immigrant editors had a voice in party councils (Jillson, 2004). Patrick Ford was given a $50,000 grant from the Republican Party to support the 1884 presidential election in the pages of the *Irish World*. As most Irish Americans supported the Democratic Party, Ford was to find ways to get them interested in the Republicans. His strategy included letting his readers know that the Irish diluted their political clout with unswerving loyalty to the Democratic Party. His argument was that this loyalty was so strong that the Democrats could ignore Irish concerns without endangering Irish support, and that the Republicans could ignore Irish concerns, convinced of the futility of wooing Irish American votes (Rodechko, 1970).

In the Northeast, the Irish were involved heavily in local politics. The Irish viewed politics as a structure of personalities, not principles; formal government was disdained by the Irish in favor of an informal (i.e., personal) impress of sovereignty. The Irish village oligarchies prepared immigrants to direct their political loyalty to those they regarded as local leaders. Many Irish voted in a bloc according to the instructions of a landlord or his agent. These traits may be loosely characterized as typical of a "machine government," which was in many respects a convergence of rural Irish custom and urban American need (Joyce, 1976). An example of Irish bloc support can be seen in the Tweed Ring in New York City in the 1860s.

William Marcy Tweed was a volunteer fireman in New York City in the 1840s, where he built a power base. He served as an alderman from 1852 to 1853 and was elected to a term in the U.S. House of Representatives. State and local affairs were his prime concern. He and a small group of men controlled New York City's finances. They dispensed jobs and contracts in return for political support and bribes. Some say that the Tweed Ring drained $30 million–$200 million from the city's resources. The Tweed Ring was successful because they were popular among many voters, especially the Irish immigrants, who received jobs and other assistance from the city government and from companies doing business with the city.[4] A series of cartoons exposing the Tweed Ring was Thomas Nast's initial campaign against corruption in government. Nast was not afraid to make direct accusations. The public outcry became unbearable. Tweed is quoted as telling Nast at one point, "Let's stop those damned pictures. I don't care so much what the papers write about me—my constituents can't read, but damn it, they can see pictures" (Paine, 1904, p. 179). A little over a year of Nast's campaign against Tweed is all it took to put a stop to Tweed, get him arrested, and put behind bars.

Ethnic Press Takes a Stand against U.S. Policy

Involvement in politics included taking a stand on issues affecting the nationalistic viewpoint of some ethnic groups within the United States. For example, in 1958, a Lebanese American journal argued that the dispatch of American Marines to Lebanon and then their quick withdrawal left the Lebanese Christians, who had demonstrated their pro-Western sentiments and friendship for America, dangerously out on a limb (Hunter, 1960).

Issues argued in the ethnic press included capitalism, prohibition, and involvement in a war. A Norwegian newspaper, *Arbeidets Ridder* published in Minneapolis by the Scandinavian Labor and Sick Benefit Society, attacked the American political parties and what they called the "capitalist press." The Swedish publication *Bokstugan* (The Book Cabin) was published in Chicago from 1910 to 1928. It was published by a Swedish and Swedish American group opposed to capitalism as well as intemperance. The German-language press was against prohibition (Hunter, 1960).

Some of the newspapers were against the United States getting involved in World War I. Irish Americans rallied to prevent American involvement in World War I because they believed that England's defeat would prepare the way for Irish independence (Carroll, 1978). Patrick Ford, editor of the *Irish World*, thought that William McKinley and the Republicans defended imperialism and this was in opposition to Catholic and Irish interests. The editor argued that Irish Americans could never tolerate imperialist endeavors that were similar to the British policies in Ireland (Rodechko, 1970).

Other ethnic newspapers spoke out about American involvement in war. The Italian newspaper *L'Appello* (The Call) published in Cleveland from 1916 to 1917 was critical of Woodrow Wilson's administration and called for general strike against the American intervention in the European war (Hoerder & Harzig, 1987). Victor Berger, born in Austria, was against the war. He purchased his first paper, the German-language *Wisconsin Vorwärts*, in 1892. Berger's most influential paper, however, was the *Milwaukee Leader*, established in 1911. The *Leader*, a popular Socialist daily, eventually became Berger's main organ for the expression of his opposition to World War I. Berger served in Congress from 1911 to 1913, the first Socialist to hold a congressional seat. He was reelected to Congress in 1919 but was denied his seat in the House because of his outspoken opposition to the United States' involvement in World War I. He was elected again and served from 1923 to 1929 (Muzik, 1964).

Other newspapers were in favor of the United States' involvement in World War I. Chicago's Czechs vigorously promoted American entrance into the war against Germany and Austria as part of the push for Czech independence. Later, after a new wave of Czech political immigrants came to Chicago in the 1960s, the Czechoslovak National Council, founded during World War I to coordinate aid to Czechoslovakia, began publishing *Vestnik* (Bulletin) to actively lobby for Czech causes in Washington during the Cold War (Cozine, 2004). There were other newspapers that expressed bitterness over the peace terms and sought to influence American opinion and American governing circles, such as the Hungarian heroes of the 1848 revolt, who published the *Szamuzottek Lappja* (Newspaper of the Exiles) (Hunter, 1960).

Prior to the war, efforts were made to create unity between the German Americans and the Germans. The German-American Alliance was formed in 1899 to rally expatriate Germans in the United States in support of Germany. The alliance had 1.5 million members in 1907. They signed an agreement with the Ancient Order of Hibernians to oppose all immigration restriction into the United States (Jillson, 2004). An important factor in inciting and sustaining the immigrants' interest in the anti-restriction campaign was the ethnic press, which teemed with lurid accounts of injustices (Jillson, 2004). The German-language press in America actively promoted the German-American Alliance as a way to boost the newspapers' declining readership; the anti-restriction campaign was supported by the newspapers.

To restrict immigration, literacy testing became part of the campaign. All male adults were excluded from admission into the United States if they were unable to read and write in their own language. The Immigration Restriction League (1894) in Boston launched a national campaign to guide public opinion toward the literacy test. A law was passed in 1895 by a huge majority. President Grover Cleveland vetoed the law in 1897. The League stayed alive, though, and pushed through a new immigration law in 1903, which authorized the deportation of foreign activists and thereby penalized newcomers for their potential opinions.

Through the active ethnic press and numerous organizations that warned against the worsening of present legislation against immigrants, the Midwest immigrant communities managed to put pressure on the president of the United States. Though the same bill passed the House and Senate in 1915, it was vetoed by President Woodrow Wilson on the basis that America should remain an asylum for the oppressed.

Propaganda

What may be nationalistic feelings to one may be propaganda to others. Polish papers were accused of being subsidized as propaganda organs for the Polish government. One of these was the Milwaukee *Kuryer Polski* (Polish Courier). The charge was vehemently denied (Olszyk, 1940). German propaganda was said to be introduced through the German-language newspapers in the United States. A. Bruno Bielaski, of the U.S. Attorney-General's office, introduced a memorandum based on photographic copies that Austria had made payments to foreign-language publications in the United States (Park, 1922); therefore, the newspapers were supported by governments outside the United States who were potential enemies as war loomed in Europe during the 1900s. And the Hungarian-language newspaper *Telegram Codzienny* (The Daily Telegram) of New York wrote in its columns: "On November 5, 1915, the Vice Consul, New York City, wrote the Austro-Hungarian Embassy that the subsidy of $700 granted to the above paper had been paid in full" (Park, 1922, p. 433). Then in 2006, the Flemish government donated €12,500 to the *Gazette van Detroit* to support the goal of enhancing the social, cultural, and commercial ties between Belgium and the United States. On its website, the newspaper maintains its independence and neutrality that the newspaper is not affiliated with any political or religious organization.[5] This still leaves a question in the minds of readers: Does who owns or pays for the press also influence information provided by the press?

In response to the charges that ethnic newspapers were publishing propaganda from other countries, the Joint Legislative Committee to Investigate Seditious Activities (commonly referred to as the Lusk Committee) sought to expose those organizations and individuals who allegedly posed a threat to American democracy and capitalism. From 1919 to 1920, throughout New York State, socialist, labor, and ethnic organizations were investigated or called before the committee to account for their activities. The Lusk Committee gathered an enormous amount of information on these groups.[6]

The information was in the form of inexpensive pamphlets, newspapers, journals, broadsides, and circulars. It was the opinion of the Lusk Committee that these forms of information generated sympathy for revolutionary philosophies among immigrant workers and other groups. The collected propaganda covered the entire spectrum of radical topics investigated by the committee including socialism and related topics (anarchism, bolshevism, communism, Marxism, etc.), capitalism, labor, pacifism, and anti-militarism. There was a wealth of material pertaining to social, economic, and political conditions in the United States, Russia, and other countries. Included were writings of Karl Marx, Frederick Engels, Nicolai Lenin, Leon Trotsky, and lesser known leaders of socialist movements in Russia and European countries.

With the escalation of verbal stands against some American policies in the ethnic press, Coleman du Pont, an industrialist who chaired the Inter-Racial Council, successor to the U.S. Chamber of Commerce's Americanization Committee, wrote: "The businessmen of America are not afraid of the truth being told, but they want it to be the truth. So we said, is the (foreign-language) press which reaches these people telling both sides of the story? Is America getting a square deal, or are the home countries and customs and traditions and institutions holding the fort? Is the American government getting a show or is it being knocked eternally?"(Sleeper, 1999, p. 10).

War brought out the best and the worst of the ethnic press. Where some newspapers spoke out against the United States being involved in any conflict, others encouraged its readers to be involved. Joining the military was one way the Irish Americans demonstrated their desire to embrace American national ideals. Irish editor John Mitchel wrote in the *Boston Pilot* that adopted citizens could pay no higher compliment or more appropriately demonstrate their "love for its institutions" or their "lofty appreciation for its freedom than by voluntarily enrolling themselves in the ranks of its defenders in the state militia" (1865, p. 1).[7]

American nationalism emerged during World War I, even among the ethnic presses. The German-language press printed the "Star-Spangled Banner" on the front pages of the 4th of July issues, urged readers to memorize the national anthem, decorated their papers with American flags, and pleaded readers to fulfill their obligations as U.S. citizens. The German-language newspapers gave free advertisement space for patriotic causes and published official information to inform their readers (Hunter, 1960).

Labor Becomes Political in America

Political involvement of the ethnic presses evolved into advocacy of issues concerning labor reform. Many ethnic groups identified themselves through the labor movement in America, especially the Irish. As the Industrial Revolution pushed its way across America, the need for cheap and abundant labor increased. More people came to America looking for jobs. The urban areas became overcrowded, and tenements were stacked with new people arriving every day. Activists like Jane Addams, who received the Nobel Peace Prize in 1931, created new settlement programs designed to conserve national holidays, customs, folksongs, and languages in the neighborhoods. Housing reform became a social issue. Danish immigrant Jacob Riis was a journalist and photographer. He exposed the horrific living conditions endured by the inhabitants of America's urban slums, which included many new immigrants. Riis' book, *How the Other Half Lives* (1890), brought about a great wave of protest and led to major housing reform in the United States.

Reform also was needed within labor. As the Industrial Revolution created jobs, it also created injustices. To fight these labor focused injustices, newspapers were created within the ethnic communities because the editors had something to say and ideas to share. It was the shared immigrant status and membership that distinguished the boundaries of the community. There were three types of labor papers: labor, radical, and reform. The labor press covered issues and argued for reforms. This press was targeted at workers, union leaders, and union members. The radical press was interested in establishing the working class as being different from other social classes and being actively opposed to other social classes. The reform press was produced for the worker by a different class, not the working class (Hoerder & Harzig, 1987).

Many ethnic newspapers advocated land reform as a solution to overcrowding in urban areas. The editors wanted cheap land freed from railroads and banks to encourage immigrants to leave the tenements and settle in the Midwest in the 1870s and 1880s. Patrick Ford, editor of the *Irish World*, urged Irish laborers to leave the urban areas and take new opportunities offered in western lands. By the late 1870s, Ford advocated Henry George's land reform program as the best remedy for economic woes.[8] Henry George was a printer and a socialist who critiqued American capitalism in his book *Progress and Poverty*.

Much of the land reform issue revolved around the ownership of large tracts of land by banks, railroad companies, and real estate dealers. These groups resold land to people at a profit, even though the Homestead Act of 1862 offered 160 acres of free land to anyone who would farm the land for 5 years. Newspapers contributed to the western migration by publishing the departing dates of groups leaving for the West from various towns so that others could join. Advertisements published in the newspapers by railroad companies were aimed at getting people to settle at certain stops along the railroad route so the company could have convenient stops, available supplies, and be able to make repairs and service the train. The land for sale promised the settler one version of the American Dream: To own a plot of land and to have a home.

To meet the demand of industry's rapid growth in the United States, a cheap supply of labor was needed, especially in the rural areas of the country. The need was largely brought on by the rapid expansion west of the American borders and was addressed by creative attempts to bring in more immigrants, and then by schemes to lure the immigrants past the traditional immigrant enclaves in coastal urban areas. Before 1820, one scheme was as redemptioners. The immigrant would contract with the captain of a ship for the cost of the trip plus 12 percent, which would be paid within 14 days after arrival. If the debt could not be paid, the captain could sell the passenger along with his wife and children for 3 to 4 years. Half of the German immigrants financed their passage in this way but only through non-German harbors such as Rotterdam and Amsterdam in the Netherlands.

Other schemes of attracting labor were through the padrone system, which involved mainly Italians and Greeks. The padrone system involved labor brokers who found immigrants from their own countries to work on the railroads, in the mines and quarries, and in agriculture. The labor brokers did more than find jobs for the immigrants; they helped with remittances, legal help when needed, and advancing transportation expenses. This system left the immigrants vulnerable because associated fees were extracted from paychecks and a padrone often controlled the wages, contracts, and food supply of the immigrants under his authority. These padroni could keep workers on the job for weeks or months beyond their contracts. Some padroni built vast labor empires, keeping thousands of workers confined in locked camps, behind barbed wire fences patrolled by armed guards (Peck, 2000). Newspapers had been the connecting points between the padrone system and the immigrants through advertisements. So in 1874, the U.S. Congress enacted the padrone statute, essentially enforcing the 13th Amendment and forbidding anyone to bring any person into the country forcibly, in confinement, or to any involuntary service. By 1882, immigrants were required to justify how they were going to provide for themselves once they arrived and prove that they would not become a public charge. This meant that they did not have to show that they were going to provide for themselves; just that someone, not the U.S. government, would be providing for them, like a husband or other family member. The Foran Act barred contract labor. Ethnic presses responded by turning their attention to the abuse of labor—not limited to recruitment, but surrounding labor reform. The newspapers advocated 8-hour workdays, elimination of fines, safety laws, a minimum working wage, a 40-hour workweek, and were against some employer policies such as accepting governmental intervention, technological change to eliminate workers, and discriminatory hiring practices. *Den Danske Pioneer* (The Danish Pioneer), published in Chicago from 1880 to 1900, supported workers' reforms, specifically the 8-hour days. Spanish and Italian newspapers also supported workers' rights. These mostly anarchist papers were dominant from the 1880s well into the 1960s (Hoerder & Harzig, 1987).

The labor reforms these papers advocated did not always turn out to be peaceful endeavors. Along with the activism parlayed through the newspapers, there was violence. Strikes often led to violence, as illustrated dramatically with the 1886 Haymarket Riot in Chicago. On the first of May, a nationwide strike was called to advocate the 8-hour workday. More than 180,000 men participated in the strike. In Chicago the number of strikers reached 60,000. Many newspapers predicted revolution and disaster, but the strikers in Chicago conducted themselves peacefully and no violence was reported. Two days later, violence broke out during a strike at the McCormick Reaper Works plant, totally unrelated to the 8-hour movement, when strikers and scabs became involved in a shoving match at the main gate. The police were called and, after being greeted by a storm of rocks, several shots were fired at the strikers. One of the strikers was killed, and five policemen were injured.

During the night, radicals at *The Alarm*, the Knights of Labor newspaper, and the *Arbeiter-Zeitung*, the daily German-language newspaper, published leaflets blaming the police for murder and calling for a mass protest meeting in Haymarket Square. The German handbill called for "annihilation for the beasts in human form who call themselves rulers. Uncompromising annihilation to them!"[9] The meeting was to take place on May 4th. A rally began about 8:30 P.M. at the Haymarket intersection in Chicago. Carter Harrison, mayor of Chicago, issued a permit for the meeting, and 1,000 people, including Harrison, turned out to listen to the protest speeches. The crowd, according to the mayor, showed no signs of revolutionary fervor. By 10 o'clock, when the last of the speakers was about to begin, only 300 people remained in the Square and Harrison left. The mayor reported to the local station that they should expect no trouble, and then he went home. The officer in charge of the police detail, Captain Bonfield, who had lost his arm during the Beer Riot of 1855, ignored the mayor's report and ordered his men to march to Haymarket Square. There, perhaps in order to instill a respect for law and order, Bonfield commanded the crowd to disperse and the 186 policemen advanced. Someone threw a bomb that landed at the head of the police column. One officer was killed, six died later, 60 others were injured. No official count was made of the civilians injured or killed. The bomber escaped (David, 1963).

Thirty-one anarchists and socialists were arrested and eight were held for trial. Four were hanged, one committed suicide, two had sentences commuted to life, and one remained in prison though there was no case against him. He was given a full pardon in 1893. The Haymarket Riot aroused strong nativist feelings against Catholics and foreign-born radicals. British newspapers blamed Irish revolutionaries for the Haymarket incident, but these reports were found to be incorrect (David, 1963). After the Haymarket bombing, 114 of the 136 exhibits at the trial were taken from Chicago's socialist and labor presses. The mainstream press in Chicago wanted to silence these socialist and labor voices. At the time there were 30,000 combined readership of the labor, socialist, and anarchist newspapers in Chicago (Reiff, 2005).

The German-language newspaper, *Arbeiter-Zeitung*, on May 4, 1886, published on the front page these headlines: "Blood! Lead and powder as a cure for dissatisfied workmen! About six laborers mortally, and four times that number slightly wounded. Thus are the eight hour men to be intimidated! This is law and order!"[10]

> The whole newspaper gang makes up the lie today that the strikers who were in the neighborhood of McCormick's factory yesterday were the first to fire. That is a bold bare faced lie, on the part of the journalistic ragamuffins. Without any warning whatever they fired at the workmen who then of course returned the fire. Indeed, why should they make so much ado about the rabble? To be sure, if they had been sheep or cattle instead of human beings, one might have reflected a little before shooting. But as it was, a laboring man is quickly replaced, and the gluttons then at their rich dinners and in the circles of their mistresses boast of the splendid achievements of law and order. In the poor shanty, miserably clad women and children are weeping for husband and father. In the palace, they touch glasses filled with costly wine and drink to the happiness of the bloody bandits of law and order. Dry your tears, ye poor and wretched; take heart, ye slaves; arise in your might and overthrow the system of robbery; present order based on robbery. (*Arbeiter-Zeitung*, 1886 May 4, p. 1)[11]

The strikes were one way to get labor reform issues heard. Other, more peaceful ways were thought to be in creating unions, which were a way to organize and to negotiate reform issues. The Knights of Labor was a national union with a large Catholic membership and leadership. The Knights emphasized cooperation between workers and owners rather than strikes. Patrick Ford, editor of the *Irish World*, favored the Knights and tried to persuade Irish Americans to avoid participation in the more aggressive American Federation of Labor (*Irish World*, 1887 Oct. 15).[12]

Many of the U.S. unions barred foreign workers from membership. These workers decided to form their own unions such as the Italian Workers Union in Houston. Many others joined the radical International Workers of the World (IWW). A Swedish immigrant, Joe Hill, born Joel Hägglund, was a member of IWW. He wrote many of the union's rallying songs. After he was executed for murder in 1914, he became the subject of folk songs himself. His 1910 song "Workers of the World" encouraged activism.

> Workers of the world awaken. Break your chains, demand your rights. All the wealth you make it taken, by exploiting parasites. Shall you kneel in deep submission from your cradle to your grave. Is the height of your ambition to be a good and willing slave? (Killebrew, 2005, para. 6)

Songs and newspaper articles fueled the controversy of labor reform. Many of the ethnic newspapers were associated with political agitation. Grievances and dissenting views repressed in the home country were often expressed in America, the home of the free. The Czech press was particularly dominant in creating fraternal periodicals; but, the first ethnic labor newspapers were published in German in the 1840s. German and Scandinavian labor periodicals were influential up to the Great Upheaval of 1880 (Hoerder & Harzig, 1987). The English and Irish did not develop a labor press of their own since they could read and contribute on this topic to the American English-language labor press. The Dutch- and French-language labor presses remained small. The Dutch remained a Christian trade union or reformist tradition press, such as the *Stemmen uit de vrije* (Voices from the Independent Dutch). This was a Unitarian-reformist newspaper in politics and devoted many articles to the working conditions and industrial disputes concerning the Dutch (Hoerder & Harzig, 1987). The depression after 1873 brought a temporary end to the French-language labor press. These reappeared from the late 1880s to the late 1920s, when the French-language labor periodicals were published in the Pennsylvania coalfields by the IWW (Hoerder & Harzig, 1987).

The focus on labor issues from the ethnic press not only often included advocating strikes but also covering strikes. Publicity about the strike activity was another function of the ethnic press, since many immigrants were involved in these labor strikes and were ethnic press readers. The tensions between the immigrant workers and Americans intensified through the pages of both the mainstream and the ethnic presses as to how the strikes were covered. When the IWW strike happened in Lawrence, Massachusetts, involving 22,000 workers of 16 nationalities, the *New York Evening Sun* wrote that "the first considerable development of an actual revolutionary spirit comes today, and comes...among the un-American immigrants from Southern Europe" (Higham, 2002). The nativist sentiment was strong among Americans in the late 1800s. In 1897, police shot into a crowd during a strike of Polish and Hungarian workers, killing 22 and wounding 40. The ethnic press reported that if the strikers had been American, no blood would have been spilled (Higham, 2002).

As the strikes continued, the ethnic press covered the deaths such as when Italian workers led strikes in cigar factories, granite quarries, and textile mills. In 1895, a group of Italian miners and residents was killed following violent strikes in the coalfields of Colorado. It involved six Italian workers and the death of an American saloon keeper. The mainstream newspapers, like *The Red Lodge (Montana) Republican Picket,* published a lengthy story on November 15, 1907, about an Italian miner who struck a mine operator over the head with a cigar clipper. This type of reporting emphasized labor violence. Press accounts frequently stressed such weapons as "foreign implements," "Italian razors," or "Montenegran stilettos" (Rolle, 1999, p. 309). These tensions between the nativist and the immigrant publicized in the press resulted in a backlash against the editors of ethnic newspapers and the immigrants. In 1912, *Il Proletario* editor Arturo Giovannitti and IWW organizer Joseph Ettor were arrested for inciting murder after Anna LoPizzo, a textile striker, was killed in Lawrence, Massachusetts. Both were found innocent. Then in Ludlow, Colorado, National Guardsmen attempted to break a miners' strike by burning down the strikers' tent village. Called the Ludlow Massacre of 1914, those killed in the fire included 56 workers, 2 women, and 11 children; all were Italian immigrants. Both presses took sides, but the stronger side was developed by the money of the Rockefeller family, who owned the coal mines in Ludlow, Colorado. They hired Ivy Lee, from Cedartown, Georgia, to set up an agency to help corporations deal with the press and to restore the Rockefeller image. Lee became known for his work in crisis management.

Summary

Politics in American immigrant communities was a lot like it had been in the home country. Many of the ethnic presses supported the revolutions, programs, and people who were still fighting the problems back home that made the immigrants leave in the first place. These nationalist newspapers also published articles against some of the U.S. policies including involvement in any European war and restrictions on immigrants entering the United States. The war in Europe caused the ethnic press in the United States to publish propaganda pertaining to the home country. Finally, the labor press became political activists as the immigrant editors fought for workers' rights.

Though many mainstream newspapers covered the issues of labor reform and were just as guilty of taking subsidies and reporting propaganda, it was the ethnic press that gave alternative views to the issues. None of the politics discussed in the ethnic press could be separated from the immigrant experience and the ethnic culture the immigrants brought to America. Ties back home were strong, as seen through the nationalistic ethnic press, but many immigrants found ways to work within the political structure of America. They critiqued the American political system, publicized the immigrant issues, and formed labor reform unions and movements to make changes in the system. Their efforts began to shape the American Dream.

[1] Quoted in *The Observer* [London] 1961, November 26.

[2] Echoes of Freedom: South Asian Pioneers in California 1899–1965. (1917, June 1). Retrieved from http://www.lib.berkeley.edu/SSEAL/echoes/chapter 7/chapter7.html.

[3] The dates of the knighting do not match the actual anniversary dates.

[4] See the Tweed Ring from http://www.u-s-history.com/pages/h703.html.

[5] See www.gazettevandetroit.com.

[6] See http://www.archives.nysed.gov/a/research/res_topics_bus_lusk.shtml.

[7] *The Boston Pilot* (1865, July 26), p. 1. Retrieved from http://catalog.mwa.org of Newsbank and the American Antiquarian Society.

[8] See the *Irish World*, September 20, 1873, p. 4; April 24, 1875, p. 4; August 4, 1877, p. 4; June 29, 1878, p. 4; October 4, 1879, p. 4; November 22, 1879, p. 4; December 27, 1879, p. 4; May 15, 1880, p. 5; June 26, 1880, p. 4; January 6, 1883, p. 4; October 13, 1883, p. 4; and March 7, 1885, p. 11. Retrieved from http://catalog.mwa.org of Newsbank; the American Antiquarian Society; & Rodechko, p. 527.

[9] See records of trial documents retrieved from http://www.loc.gov/teachersclass roommaterials/connections/haymarket/langarts3.html for the following: People's Exhibit 63, Arbeiter-Zeitung (Newspaper), "Blood," 1886 May 4 (pages 8 and 9).

[10] Quote is attributed to Michael Schwab in court documents filed during the Haymarket trials. See the Illinois Supreme Court Decision in the Haymarket Case (1887) *Illinois vs. August Spies et al.* Illinois Supreme Court, Writ of error decision, 1887, September 14., Volume O, 172–389, 220 p. Opinion by Magruder, J. Retrieved from http://www.law.umkc.edu/faculty/projects /Ftrials/haymarket/haymarketillsct.html.

[11] See *Illinois vs. August Spies et al.* trial evidence book. People's Exhibit 63. *Arbeiter-Zeitung* (Newspaper, "Blood," 1886, May 4). Retrieved from http:// www.chicagohs.org/hadc/tranSCRIPT/exhibits/X051-100/X061A.htm.

[12] Retrieved from http://catalogue.mwa.org of Newsbanks and the American Antiquarian Society.

Chapter Eight /
Literary Mission: Belles-Lettres

Di prese iz a melukhe far zikh—
The press is a kingdom unto itself.
Yiddish expression

The Yiddish expression captures the influence of the newspapers in providing information for enlightenment. The intellectual came to America for many reasons. Some came as a result of religious or political persecution. Others came because they were censored or restricted from writing on topics they were passionate about. Regardless of what they did full-time to make a living, most of the intellectuals edited newspapers or wrote for newspapers on the side. The intellectual brought to the immigrant community the idealism of a better world, a world of freedom, brotherhood, and equality. The intellectual fed the spirit of the American Dream where anything could happen, that there was a better, more beautiful world, and it could be theirs.

The intellectual voice was colored with belle-lettres (fine letters), literature that is appreciated for the beauty, artistry, and originality of its style and tone rather than for its ideas and informational content. In the ethnic presses of America, the intellectuals shared both the belle-lettres of their culture and the intellectual ideas through criticism and essays.

Though language was important in communicating the literature of the home country, intellectual ideas needed the language even more to enable the editor to communicate with peasant immigrants. For example, Yiddish was learned by many intellectual Jewish writers so they could communicate with the workers on social and labor reforms. Immigrants were working hard jobs with long hours. There was no time even to think about issues, yet reforms were needed to help the immigrants reach toward that dream of a better life. The newspaper function extended from teaching the people how to read to teaching them how to think. Education was advocated, and to pull the reader into the newspaper, the intellectuals offered the immigrants memories of the home country through the belle-lettres as well as new ideas for social and labor reforms. The memories were fostered through serialized novels in the newspapers and reflected on the loneliness and isolation the immigrants felt in America.

The newspapers and journals founded and edited by many of these intellectuals were not always successful ventures. Those that were successful found that the readers wanted more fiction, literature, and a discussion of issues. Once these readers assimilated into American life and culture and could read English, editors felt the need for the ethnic press, as it existed then, lessened, so they provided an arena for more complex or nuanced discussions of their collective circumstances. For example, the Cotter's Son serial published in 1899 saved the Norwegian newspaper in Iowa, *Decorah Posten*, from bankruptcy. This newspaper also ran the comic strip "Han Ola Og Han Per" drawn by Peter Julius Rosendahl from 1918 to 1935 (Lovoll, 1977). Newspapers began to include satire, humor, and political cartoons. As early as 1895, Richard Felton Outcault's "Micky Dugan" was published in the *New York World*. Micky Dugan was an Irish slum urchin who wore a bright yellow shirt, so the comic strip was known as "The Yellow Kid" (Outcault, 1995). Finley Peter Doone wrote a weekly column called "Mr. Dooley" for the *Chicago Evening Post* beginning in 1893. He poked fun using an Irish brogue. For example, he wrote in 1902:

> The newspaper does ivrything fr us. It runs th' polis force an' th' banks, commands th' milishery, controls th' ligislachure, baptizes th' young, marries th' foolish, comforts th' afflicted, afflicts th' comfortable, buries th' dead an' roast him afterward. (Doone, 1902, p. 240)

Issues discussed included temperance, Anglo American prejudice toward foreigners, corruption in politics, slaveholding, land acquisition, and urban growth. The fiction and poetry was about the homeland and nostalgia. Many of the intellectuals wrote about their losses of cultural influence and political power. At times the intellectual voice was important enough to the immigrants that money was raised to buy the intellectual passage to America.

Intellectuals who came to America brought with them their discontent and interest in revolutionary ideals. These ideals had been adopted from the socialism of the French Revolution, the communism of Marx and Engels, and the European revolutions of 1848. Social change was being advocated, and the intellectuals were the voices being heard. Arturo Giovannitti, an Italian intellectual, had his first poem published in the May Day edition of *Il Proletario*, the Italian-language newspaper of the International Workers of the World (IWW).

There were many voices. At one time there were 50 Finnish American publishers of belle-lettres. Other immigrant groups did not include belle-lettres in their newspapers for a long time after settlement in America. For example, the Norwegians were here for 50 years before any notable works of literary fiction were produced. These immigrants spent their energies on conquering the land, and after that they concentrated on building a new social order. With the arrival of the Forty-Eighters from Germany, these revolutionaries initiated literary and musical societies, freethinker movements, gymnastic organizations as well as newspapers (Rippley, 1976). Half of the Forty-Eighters were active in journalism (Wittke, 1957). And, at one time, a majority of all German-language newspapers in the United States were controlled by Forty-Eighters. There were many literary voices in America during this time of great immigration; however, voices chosen to illustrate the belle-lettres in ethnic newspapers include the Chinese, Czechs, Germans, Hungarians, Jews, Lithuanians, and Swedish. These illustrate the literary hopes intellectuals brought to America for their own interpretation of the American Dream.

Chinese

Jingshan Xinwenlu (Golden Hill News) was the first Chinese-language newspaper in the United States, published in San Francisco, April 22, 1854 (Yin, 2003). As is typical with ethnic newspapers, it published shipping news, commodity prices, local news and news from Chinese provinces. To promote circulation, most Chinese-language newspapers had some form of literary work. Two notable newspapers known for their literary contributions and influence within the Chinese American enclaves were the *Chung Sai Yat Pao* (China-West Daily), founded in 1900 by Ng Poon Chew, an eminent Chinese journalist, and *Mon Hing Yat Bo* (Chinese World), to which Sui Sin Far (Edith Maude

Eaton, 1865–1914), the first Chinese American woman writer, contributed (Yin, 2003).

The *San Francisco China News* was published by John P. Bogardus and Frank L. Gordon in 1874. As a literary newspaper, the entire newspaper was handwritten except for the logo, with no authors named. Though there were many dialects in Chinese, the literate Chinese could all read the same characters; therefore, Chinese-language publications, called Report Papers, reinforced the ethnic consciousness and solidarity of Chinese immigrants (Yin, 2003).

Each of the Chinese-language newspapers had a special section called the "fukan," which were the literary pages. With the revitalization of Chinese-language newspapers in the United States in the 1970s, these literary sections gained new importance with Chinese writers publishing their work in serial form before they were published in book form in Asia. Yin (2003) offers examples: Yu Lihua's best seller *Sons and Daughters of the Fu Family*, which deals with the experiences of Chinese student immigrants in America, was a big hit when it first appeared in serial form in *Xingdao Ribao* (Sing Tao Daily) in New York in 1976. *Breaking Out*, a popular novel by Chen Ruoxi on Chinese immigrants in San Francisco, was brought out in serial form in *Shijie Ribao* (Chinese American Daily) throughout the United States in 1982 prior to its publication in Hong Kong, Taipei, and Beijing in 1983. *The American Moon*, a best seller by Cao Youfang about Chinese restaurant workers in New York, stimulated strong interest among Chinese readers throughout North America when it was serialized in 1985 in *Zhong Bao* (Central Daily) in New York.

Czechs

Czechs brought with them to America the free thought movement and a developed literary culture (Hoerder & Harzig, 1987). The free thought movement involved Czechs who had split from the Catholic Church and who believed in mankind, nature, and the universe. There was no structure to its denomination, building, or services. They believed in love, justice, science, and art. *Pokrok*, a weekly publication for Freethinkers, established in 1867 in Cleveland, Ohio, claimed itself to be for religious independents. *Slovan Amerikansky* was a Freethinkers' newspaper in

Wisconsin as early as 1860; Chicago had *Svornost*. These newspapers and others were said to be edited by freethinking intellectuals who stressed Slavonic culture and the Czech language (Nelson, 1992).

Germans

Sunday editions of German-language newspapers were called Sonntagsblätter. These editions were essentially articles copied verbatim from other periodicals with no credit given or royalties provided. They included essays, novels, humorous stories, and serials.

One newspaper said to be so good that other newspapers copied it was *Alte und Neue Welt*, the voice of the German liberals in 1830. A group of ex-revolutionaries met at the Lafayette Hotel in Philadelphia and discussed issues to be published in the newspaper. Edited by Johann Georg Wesselhöf until 1834, the newspaper was concerned about the social and cultural activities of the Philadelphia Germans. Always on the first page were parts of novels, poems, biographies, and other literary material chosen from the best in the field of German belle-lettres. The choices published helped to set a high standard (Wittke, 1957).

Wilhelm Eichthal published *Deutsche Schnellpost* in 1843 in New York. The newspaper was considered to be devoted primarily to politics, science, and literature. Isidor Busch, in 1849, published *Israels Herold* in New York. Busch was an intellectual Forty-Eighter who had published revolutionary tracts in Vienna in 1848. His newspaper failed after three months because it was considered too literary and philosophical for the average reader and too liberal for the orthodox (Wittke, 1957). German foreign-language newspapers were known for their wit and humor. An example was *Die Lokomotive* published in 1853 in New York by Adolph Strodtmann. As an illustrated comic, it was published weekly but lost money quickly and closed. The *Frischer Lunch* newspaper poked fun at German Americans and was published in New York in 1859 (Wittke, 1957).

Other examples of German-language belle-lettres included the work of Rudolf Lexow, having worked for the *Police Gazette* newspaper; he founded the *New Yorker Criminal Zeitung und Belletristisches Journal*. The journal grew from 20,000 circulation in 1855 to 71,500 in 1880. It ceased publication in 1911. The journal reprinted selections from the world's great literature, from Johann Wolfgang von Goethe to Harriet Beecher Stowe and from Dumas to Thackeray, as well as original fiction. In 1875, Udo Brachvogel became the associate editor of the journal after leaving the St. Louis *Westliche Post.* As a writer of ballads, he published Bret Harte's early stories, German novels in serial form, and translations from French and English authors. His readers demanded more fiction. To raise the magazine's literary standards, Julius Goebel replaced Brachvogel as editor of the newspaper. Goebel left the Johns Hopkins University to edit the newspaper, but after three years, he had failed to get additional readers. The journal staff did what many ethnic papers tried to do when declining circulations and advertising were threatening to close them down—they tried to compete with commercial papers. The headlines got bolder and more news was printed with less literature (Wittke, 1957).

An example of a German-language newspaper that appeared similar to commercial mainstream newspapers was the *Deutech-Amerikanische Monatshefte für Politik, Wissenschaft und Literature* in Chicago edited by Casper Butz in the 1860s. The content included discourses on the nature of matter, immigration, labor, a universal language, art, politics, poetry, novels, and book reviews (Wittke, 1957). Notable German American contributors included Johann Stallo, Carl Schurz, Franz Sigel, and Reinhard Solger. Many of the German-language writers in 19th-century America were journalists who wrote fiction as a sideline. During the 20 years that preceded the Civil War, these writers often serialized their novels in the German-language press, often writing with considerable local color about the particular places in America where they had settled. Rudolf Lexow wrote about New York, Heinrich Boernstein about St. Louis, and Emil Klauprecht about Cincinnati (Adams, Reichmann & Rippley, 1993).

One of the writers published in Butz's newspaper, Carl Schurz, was a hero of the failed German revolution. Schurz mirrored Friedrich Hecker's involvement in politics and immigration. After the war, Schurz was the Washington correspondent for the *New York Tribune.* Then he was editor-in-chief of the *Detroit Post,* but he left to become the editor of the German-language newspaper the *Westliche Post* in St. Louis, Missouri, where one of his close friends was Joseph Pulitzer. He was appointed secretary of the interior by President Rutherford Hayes. After leaving this office in 1881, he returned to journalism and became managing editor of the *New York Evening Post*. He also wrote for *Harper's Weekly* and *The Nation* and had several books published including *The Life of Henry Clay* (1887) and *Abraham Lincoln* (1891) (Schurz, 1907). As a member of the press, he was able to use such standing to affect change on American politics and impact the American Dream.

Hungarians

Hungarian American writing, though patriotic, portrayed a deep longing the immigrants had for the home country. The poets, writers, and intellectuals fed these immigrant feelings of fear and alienation through the literature published in the newspapers. The immigrants learned that their lives were made easier by participating in the activities of their churches, other organizations, and by reading Hungarian-language newspapers. Four poets contributed greatly to the contemporary Hungarian-language newspapers: Györgu Kemény (wrote *András Vas*), László Szabó (wrote heroic epics and was known for his adept portrayal of the sea), Árpád Tarnócy (respected lyricist and founding editor of *Akroni Magyar Hírlap* / Arkron Hungarian Journal), and László Pólya.

Pólya had a Juris Doctorate from the University of Budapest. At 29, full of adventure and also involved in politics, he came to America. He worked at the mines in Ohio and then became a frequent contributor to major newspapers such as the New York *Amerikai Magyar Népazava* (American Hungarian People's Voice) and the Cleveland *Szabadság* (Liberty). Restless, he always traveled with just a suitcase and did not settle down nor take a permanent position with any Hungarian-language newspaper. He lectured, wrote, sat and drank wine, and talked with people. He wrote about his abandoned home country and his love of everything Hungarian (Várdy, 1985).

Many of the Hungarian literary societies included members who were left-leaning, highly sophisticated, urbane intellectuals who sorely missed the intellectual atmosphere of Budapest. Two of these societies were the Ady Endre Társaság (Ady Endre

Society) and the Kultúr Szövetség (Cultural Federation). Newspapers were often a product of these literary societies. In 1879, William Loew and Arkád Mogyórossy, two literary Hungarians, began the newspaper the *Magyar Amerika* (Hungarian America). The newspaper failed after just a few issues, in all likelihood because it was too intellectual for the Hungarian immigrants at that time (Várdy, 1985).

Most of the Hungarian immigrant writers made their living by editing or writing for Hungarian-language newspapers. One such writer was József Reményi, who after writing for Hungarian-language newspapers, became a lecturer (1929) and then professor of comparative literature at Western Reserve University in Cleveland, Ohio. He was the first significant interpreter of Hungarian literature to American audiences (Várdy, 1985). Another Hungarian writer was Pál Szarvas (1883–1938); he wrote for a Pittsburgh newspaper under the pseudonym of Indian. His simple weekly rhymes (Heti Strófák) were about the tragedies and comedies of Hungarian American life during the 1920s and 1930s. Szarvas was widely read by the workers (Várdy, 1985).

Jewish / Yiddish

The vitality of the socialist Yiddish press in the 1890s attracted a steadily increasing number of intellectuals to Yiddish journalism. Many Jewish intellectuals spoke only Russian. They were urged to take up Yiddish because Russian could only reach a small section of intellectuals while Yiddish could be used to reach thousands of workers (Michels, 2000). Many of the Russian Jews thought, however, that the Russian language indicated their status as intellectuals. An immigrant named Max Podell writes in an unpublished autobiography, "How I envied those Russian intelligencia [sic]! They were always at the top of every social function, the attraction of every circle and the ideal of every girl's dreams" (Michels, 2000, p. 66).

During the same time frame, there were aspiring writers who lacked knowledge of Russian, English, or German. They represented a stratum of self-educated intellectuals who rose to positions of leadership in the labor movement and earned respect in the Yiddish literary world (Michels, 2000). The intellectual editor thought it was his service to educate his readers. One edi-

tor for the *Arbeiter-Zeitung* even wrote a column where he criticized rejected manuscripts just for the benefit of the writers
(Hunter, 1960). Newspapers were important to the Jewish intellectual. Abraham Cahan said, "For us [the *Volkszeitung*] was a
real treasure....This newspaper was the reason some of us
learned German even before we learned English. It played a
major role in our intellectual development" (Cahan, 1969, p. 227).

The Yiddish literary movement of the 1920s in America included the poets Moyshe-Leyb Halpern and Moshe Nadir, and
writer Isaac Raboy. These writers were committed to political
radicalism and were published in the newspapers *Freiheit*
(Communist) and *Freie Arbeiter Shtimme* (anarchist) (Buhle,
1989). Halpern was a staff poet at *Freiheit* in 1922. Critic
Noyakh Shtaynberg wrote that "He sings from his blood and his
blood is of revolution" (Levinson, 2004, p. 143). Yiddish newspapers published for the educated Jews included *Auflau* (Reconstruction). Published in 1934, the newspaper included drama and
literature (Hunter, 1960). Another Yiddish paper, the *Yuedishe
Zeitung* (Jewish Times) published all aspects of politics, religion,
history, science, and art in 1870 (Madison, 1976).

Three major Jewish intellectuals and authors, all born in the
same region of Russia in the late 19th century established a Hebrew printing press in New York. These authors illustrated the
Jewish American literary scene, the Hebrew press in America,
and the complex relation between print and society. The first
author was Eliakum Zunser, the foremost wedding bard in Jewish Eastern Europe. He was recognized as a founder of popular
poetry in Yiddish. The second intellectual author was Shomer
Nahum Meir Sheikevitsh, who is credited with inventing the
popular novel in Yiddish. He dominated the literary market he
created, authoring more than 300 novels and some 50 plays in
his short lifetime. The third author was Avraham Chaim Rosenberg, a controversial rabbi, who believed in the revolutionary
synthesis of old and new as demonstrated in his store of scholarly works (Blondheim, 1997).

All three of these men, though they had been accomplished
and well-known authors in the literary and scholarly environment of Jewish Eastern Europe, were revolutionary and controversial in their home country. However, when the three

immigrated to America with the wave of East European Jews seeking refuge from deteriorating economic conditions, political oppression, and physical danger late in the 19th century and early in the 20th, they became even less known as scholars. To be productive, they had to make a living as printer-publishers. Their literary and spiritual uprooting, being transplanted into a new land, made it necessary for them to establish and to help shape a new world of letters in America.

Lithuanians

From 1914 to 1939 there were more Lithuanians in Chicago than in Lithuania's capital of Vilnius. This resulted in developing a dozen Lithuanian parishes, three daily newspapers, and a Lithuanian opera company. Most Lithuanian publishers were based in Chicago (the first Lithuanian book in Chicago was published in 1880). Between 1892 and 1974, about 90 Lithuanian newspapers and magazines were founded in Chicago (Balys, 1976). Though the first Lithuanian immigrants had modest educations, they were energetic and eager for success, which meant they were self-educated. Many of these Chicago Lithuanians attended Valparaiso University in Indiana. Others were avid readers, despite the long working hours (6 days a week, 10–12 hours daily). Between 1875 and 1910 some 1,350 books and pamphlets in Lithuanian were printed in the United States. They were mostly translations of stories, hymnals and songbooks, popularized science, historical works, and novels (Balys, 1976).

Swedish

In the United States the Swedish publication *Bokstugan* (The Book Cabin), a periodical of the adult education movement, issued from 1919 to 1926 by the Verdandi Study League, recruited many of its members from the anarchists who found a home in the Industrial Workers of the World, a radical union. Promoted as a cultural journal, it had anarchist, communist, and socialist contributors. Much of the content was creative writing and included stories, plays, literary criticism, and scientific articles. There were articles on broader aspects of politics including some that were anti-religious. Reproductions of paintings and other works of art were regularly published as were book reviews. Prominent authors in Sweden contributed to the journal including Ellen Key, Carl Lindhagen, and Erik Lindorm (Bekken, 1995). These authors set the tone of the journal.

Ellen Key (1849–1926) was a Swedish author, critic, and ideologue. She believed that women were primarily meant to be mothers; she deplored feminist claims to equality within the labor market. Her ideas regarding state child support influenced social legislation in several countries. Carl Lindhagen (1919–1940) supported female suffrage and social reform, and he advocated disarmament and international co-operation based on international law. He actively worked for a joint Scandinavian effort to promote international civil law. Lindhagen was a prominent member of the radical peace movement. Erik Lindorm (1889–1941), a Swedish poet, wrote the poem *Moment of Happiness,* published in *Bokstugan* (Bekken, 1995).

Other Swedish newspapers published articles on issues advocating rationalism, eugenics, economic equality, and individual freedom. They omitted temperance and sexual freedom but included theory and argument. An example was the Swedish newspaper *Revolt,* published in Chicago from 1911 to 1916 (Bekken, 1995). Another journal, *AHJO* (The Forge), was published by the Work People's College in Duluth, Minnesota, from 1915 to 1921. Originally a socialist workers' school, it became an International Workers of the World union supporter. Editors included both teachers and students from the school. Published as a socialist-scientific literary paper, it included many translated articles, photos, drawings, jokes, advertisements, and poems (Bekken, 1995).

Calendars

One way publishers put literature in the hands of all their readers was through its annual calendar. These calendars offering a sampling of the latest political arguments, recent fiction, and hints for decorating provided a sense of community to radicals and a sense of shared purpose and culture. Most of all, the calendars offered a fully developed alternative to mainstream American life.

The cultural task of the calendar was described best in an article published in German in 1886:

There are in fact books which are found in the poorest huts and which are therefore best suited to fulfill the mission of educating and enlightening the people: they are the calendars. A calendar is probably to be found in the most straitened household, and in some families it is the only source of intellectual stimulation for the whole year. Therefore, it is here that the lever should be applied, in order to have a meaningful effect on the education of the lower classes. (Poore, 1992, p. 110)

Calendars offered a preponderance of information about the lives, tastes, political preferences, cultural activities, and aspirations of the first generation immigrants by summarizing their history as seen by the immigrants themselves (Várdy, 1985). Calendars followed a similar format regardless of the sponsoring group. First was a picture on the title page or a reproduction of a painting. Next would be the calendar section with illustrations for each month of the year and lists of important dates from both American and European history. Following this list would be an annual poem to introduce the big reading section. At the end of the calendar there were advertisements and greetings from organizations in major towns and lists of books that could be ordered (Poore, 1992).

In America, both the German- and Hungarian-language newspapers produced calendars for their readers. For the German-language readers, the calendars were most often published by the German American radical press, who maintained the political community through the calendars. For the Hungarian-language readers, calendars had been a part of Hungarian life since 1626 (Várdy, 1985).

In the year 1931, a Hungarian American calendar included 194 pages. Twenty-nine pages were devoted to the calendar. Of the remaining 165 pages, 33 were advertisements and 132 were essays, short stories, and poems. Of the 25 essays, 8 were on topics of general information, 4 on history, and 13 on various aspects of Hungarian American life. The literary section of these calendars was important to the immigrants in retaining the memories of home: "Their eternal longing for the never-never land of the Mother Country that continues to live and to grow in their imagination is an ever-present and ever-recurring theme of these essays" (Várdy, 1985, p. 81).

Summary

    The intellectuals who shared their ideas with each other and with the workers and peasants in America helped to create a new function of the ethnic press: enlightenment. The intellectuals offered the immigrants memories of their home country. Ethnic newspapers showcased the best literary talent of their people. The newspapers strove to educate their readers through the ideas discussed and reforms advocated. The writers in these literary sections of the newspapers were seen as heroes, superiors, and intellectuals who could lead the people to think a particular thought, and that thought was education so they would have a better life, another development of the American Dream.

Part III /
Challenges and the Road Ahead

Editors and publishers of ethnic presses came to the United States with barriers already in place against being successful in the publishing business. Most of the editors and publishers had no background in publishing. They, too, experienced the loneliness and isolation of having left their homelands and experienced the language difficulties within the new country. Immigrant problems aside, these editors and publishers had additional problems to overcome, such as rivalries, competition within the ethnic communities, the large anti-immigrant movement in the United States with any new wave of immigration and decline of economic opportunity. These editors and publishers also had to work with the changes taking place within the ethnic communities as the members of the communities move through the stages of acculturation, assimilation, and cultural pluralism.

Chapter Nine /
Fundamental Internal Press Issues

The newspapers! Sir, they are the most villainous,
licentious, abominable, infernal—not that I ever read them!
No, I make it a rule never to look into a newspaper.
Richard Brinsley Sheridan (1908, p. 9)

"Fight!" some might shout and people would crowd around to see what was happening. A good fight was worth talking about. Editors of ethnic presses fought. They fought each other over circulation, politics, and ideals. In spite of the fact that newspapers were an integral part of the immigrant community and used to link the immigrant's home country with the new country, there were many problems the immigrants brought with them to America. Together, the issues, new and old, helped to form the ethnic presses. Though the functions of the press encouraged the immigrant to look back and to look forward, there were tensions within the ethnic communities that were displayed in the pages of the ethnic presses. The tensions were exacerbated by the fact that the editors and publishers were often so much a part of the community that the community could not be separated from the editors' philosophy, and some editors were passionate about certain issues. Other editors and publishers feuded with rivals to gain circulation and thus remain profitable. Not surprisingly, plenty of editors and publishers accepted publishing as a business and treated it as such. Business or not, the ethnic press transferred the home country rivalries and political disputes to the United States. The newspapers took these problems on and exploited them to the fullest. It was every man for himself—more true insomuch as there were few women in journalism in the early years of immigration.

The problems facing the ethnic press in the United States included the business angle of how to attract readers and how to fund the newspapers. Other internal problems were the intense rivalries between editors of presses within an ethnic group. And finally, the perception of the ethnic newspapers and their editors from outside the ethnic community often was negative. Ethnic newspapers were perceived by mainstream journalists as second class periodicals, with no real advertising base, limited circulation, and delivered only to the ethnic communities with language-specific needs. These newspapers were seen as coming from a politically downtrodden people—immigrants—and included few women. In most instances, the perception was correct.

Newspapers as a Business

A challenge to ethnic newspaper editors, who approached the newspaper as a business, was the audience. Readers were limited often to members of one ethnic group, especially if the language was not English. The Irish, British, Australians, West Indians and others who could read English would read the English-language newspapers, but would also have an ethnic newspaper for important news from home and the community not found in the mainstream press. These ethnic groups formed clusters mostly in urban areas and in some small towns, though immigrants were scattered all through the West. Finding the readers was easier in the concentrated urban areas, but as the westward expansion pulled the immigrants away, finding readers became a struggle and an expense for the ethnic press. Additional reader challenges included the high rate of illiteracy among the early immigrants even in their own language. Groups, like the Norwegians, focused first on making a success on the farm before they turned to literary issues, so the Norwegian presses were late in forming. At the bottom of the immigrants' barrel—illiterate and poor like the Irish and Italians—these immigrants found it hard just to make a living much less buy and read a newspaper.

Ethnic newspapers began with high hopes for the editors and publishers, who had a vision and wanted to share it with their people. Some editors thought it was their duty to educate their country people on issues and ideas. These editors soon discovered that the early immigrants were concerned more about local issues, especially those that would affect them and their ability to get ahead. Others were too tired, too poor, too battered to take seriously the issues spouted in the various ethnic newspapers. Some of the publishers who started with optimism would then end with cynical comments about fickle readers who lacked the courage to support a principle. Money was an important part of the ethnic press business and was found in different ways. The newspaper could be financed by an individual or association—publishing association, fraternal organization, or religious institution—or through subscriptions, advertising, and subsidies.

Individual owners of ethnic newspapers were strong and dedicated personalities who were often willing to take financial risks for their papers, which they viewed as an essential community service. Plus, an added advantage was that the owners could dictate editorial policy, a feature challenged by German editors who frequently quarreled with their newspaper's owners. These editors resented every attempt to interfere with their freedom of expression, insisting that the editor's principles, and not the publisher's wishes, should determine the character and content of the paper (Wittke, 1957).When the owners saw the paper as a business enterprise, they allowed the editors great latitude in editorial policy as long as the editors maintained circulation and the newspaper was profitable. Patrick Donahoe, publisher of the *Boston Pilot*, allowed a succession of editors to dictate the editorial policy of the newspaper. This resulted in an erratic editorial policy and sometimes a hostile relationship with the Catholic hierarchy. Patrick Ford, editor of the *Irish World*, wrote that there was no daily Irish paper because the Irish read English. He further cited the expense that daily publishing would involve. Such expense would force a paper to find a financial patron. "But a pensioned paper never can, and never should, have any influence with the people. The very fact of its dependency on a political 'ring' or clique for support would destroy its power for good" (Rodechko, 1970, p. 524).

Newspapers were sponsored by publishing associations developing from within a political or religious organization, union, or institution. A membership to the group would include a subscription to the newspaper. At times the official newspaper of an association would cause great tensions within the ethnic community. For example, the Hungarian American communities feuded about everything, but particularly the custom of associations and fraternities selecting an official newspaper. Circulation based on membership to an organization guaranteed an audience and financial support but caused Hungarian-language newspapers to wage intensive and emotional campaigns for the endorsements from local associations and fraternities. Despite the benefits such endorsements could bring, they also opened up the possibility that the membership and especially the leadership would have a voice in the editorial policy of the newspaper. It also risked the professional standards of the newspapers since the editors had to cater to the larger membership of the organization (Várdy, 1985).

German-language newspapers also were forced to conform. Many of the newspapers received political party subsidies, which resulted in abuse of the information published to conform to the political principles of the party. Editors would adjust their political principles to conform to the wishes of the highest bidder (Wittke, 1957).

Advertising and subscriptions were other ways through which publishers and owners funded their newspapers. Wilhelm Weitling started the newspaper *Die Republik der Arbeiter*, in 1850 in New York City. His goal was total reconstruction of the social order. He began by knocking on doors, going from house to house among the New York Germans, and he secured 400 subscribers in 4 days. He solicited the aid of agents and followers in the larger cities to help build circulation for his paper. He personally went on several propaganda tours to share his program and to solicit subscriptions. Though he lost 200 subscribers after the first issue was published, he gained 250 new readers. By the third issue he had 2,000 and by the end of the first year he had 4,000 subscribers. How many were actually paid subscriptions is not clear. Though the newspaper lasted 5 years, after the summer of 1851, the newspaper was in serious financial trouble. Copies mailed to other cities were not sold. The editor had a long illness of typhoid combined with long propaganda tours of acting editors, which resulted in financial instability for the newspaper (Wittke, 1957).

Advertising did not work for the Irish. Patrick Ford, editor of the *Irish World*, did not consider advertising practical for an Irish American paper:

> An Irish daily could not count much on legitimate advertisements. There is a stupid prejudice existing in the minds of many Anglo-Americans that forbids them to patronize anything having an Irish or Catholic complexion....Quite a number of the heaviest Protestant business men are deacons in the church, and they might think, perhaps, that any patronage ex-

tended to a Catholic paper, even in a business way, would be aiding Popery. (Rodechko, 1970, p. 540)

Subsidies were thought to be another way to finance a newspaper. Immigrant editors over and over again felt they were justified in taking subsidies. For example, James V. Donnaruma, editor of *La Gazzetta del Massachusetts* on April 7, 1936, sent a letter to Giovanni M. DiSilvestro, director of the Italian-American Division of the Foreign Language Bureau of the Republican National Committee. In the letter Donnaruma suggested that his involvement in the Republican Party campaigns made him believe that he should be rewarded financially for his endorsements. He wrote: "National advertising should be given to newspapers that have been doing work for the Republican Party in the past years" (Deschamps & Luconi, 2002, p. 126).

Monies were sought by newspaper editors through contributions and patronage as a way to produce the newspaper when there were not enough advertising revenues or subscriptions. Cairoli Gigliotte, the former editor of *The Newcomer*, a defunct Chicago-based Italian American newspaper, offered GOP presidential candidate Herbert Hoover his support to conduct an education campaign for Republican policies if Hoover would give Gigliotte $10,000 to resume publication. In 1940, Joseph J. Lunghino, publisher of Buffalo, New York's *Il Corriere Italiano*, informed the Republican State Committee that he had published many releases from the Republican National Committee and should be included in the list of publications that would carry the state and national political advertisements (Deschamps & Luconi, 2002). The Chinese-language newspaper in San Francisco, the *World Journal*, was financed through subsidies given by reformers seeking to depose the Empress Dowager in China (Zhou & Cai, 2002). And the Hungarian-language newspaper in New York, *Amerikai Magyar Népszava* (American Hungarian People's Voice) edited by Géza D. Berkó, was given a direct subsidy from the Hungarian government to champion Hungarian national interests in America (Wittke, 1957).

Financial problems were not the only problems. Among many of the ethnic communities, it was difficult to find enough trained journalists, editors, and businessmen to keep the papers publishing. The Catholic press complained about the lack of competent editors. Many of the newspapers were visions of single individuals who took the risks to get their views, poetry, and ideas out through their own publications.

Rivalries

Editors of the ethnic press appeared to forget all journalism values when their ire was raised. L. Stierlin, editor of *Anzeiger* in 1851, published a picture of a jackass on the cover of the newspaper. The jackass was labeled as a portrait of Anton Eickhoff, editor of the rival *Beobachter am Ohio* (Wittke, 1957). Editors indulged in personal abuse and engaged in disgraceful feuds, including threats to horsewhip their rivals. Vile expletives took the place of argument, and overstatement and even slander was common (Wittke, 1957). *Il Progresso Italo-Americano* in New York from 1880 to 1988 engaged in vicious personal polemics with its rivals that frequently resulted in physical attacks or lawsuits (Vecoli, 1983).

The strongest rivalries were among editors of the same ethnic group but with different points of view either about politics or religion. The longest argument among newspaper editors may have been between the nationalists and the Catholics within the Irish American communities. The Catholic Church condemned the nationalists for trying to overthrow a legitimate government and criticized the nationalists for distracting Irish Americans from more important American concerns, such as the challenge presented by the Know-Nothing movement. The Irish American press split into warring camps, with papers adopting a nationalist viewpoint of freeing Ireland or a Catholic outlook of forging ahead (Joyce, 1976). The two presses unified during the 1870s when Patrick Donahoe, owner of the *Boston Pilot*, appointed John Boyle O'Reilly as editor. O'Reilly was an ex-Fenian convert to Home Rule.

This argument between the nationalists and the Catholics resulted after the failed Young Ireland revolt. Many leaders of the Young Ireland movement migrated to the United States. Once here, they created new types of newspapers to reflect their own embattled point of view of the political situation in Ireland. These new editors were hostile to Catholics. The Catholics were equally quick to reciprocate the suspicion and mistrust aimed at them. Each side blamed the other for the disastrous conditions in Ireland at the time, particularly for the collapse of the Young Ireland movement and the jailing or forced exiling of their leaders. The press entered a new era of contention and conflict. There were four editors who brought this conflict to life in the Boston and New York communities. These four editors were Thomas D'Arcy McGee, James A. McMaster, Patrick Lynch, and John Roddan. All four had specific points of view on the issue. McGee and Lynch advocated the point of view of the nationalists, and McMaster and Roddan supported the viewpoint of the Catholics. All of these arguments were going on during the same time period: 1840–1850s.

McGee started *The Nation* in New York as a duplicate of the newspaper he had worked on in Ireland as part of the Young Ireland movement. He was devoted to the Irish and European revolutions as well as immigrant education. His feuding with the Catholic point of view began as a response to articles Bishop John Hughes had published in his newspaper the *Freeman's Journal* in New York. This argument over the failed Young Ireland movement and the involvement of the Catholic Church eventually led McGee into another feud but this time with James McMaster (Joyce, 1976). McMaster bought the *Freeman's Journal* from Bishop Hughes and vowed to hold up the principles of the bishop and regarded himself as a "representative and defender of Catholic truth in a world of passion and corruption" (Kwitchen & McMaster, 1949, p. 82). His main target was McGee. McMasters said McGee was "spiteful against Catholic priests" and hostile to his own people, whom he was accused of characterizing as "the dung of the church" (Joyce, 1976, p. 59). McGee fought back through the newspaper articles and columns. McMaster edited the *Freeman's Journal* for 38 years. His Catholic viewpoint influenced many Irish Americans. The crisis encouraged McGee finally to flee to Boston (Joyce, 1976).

Patrick Donahoe owned the *Boston Pilot*. His mission, as he saw it, was to assist in the liberation of Ireland. Initially, his strong national sentiment was not challenged by the *Boston Catholic Observer*. However, the challenge was met in the summer of 1848 when Father O'Brien's *Observer* accused the *Boston Pilot* of heresy and consorting with radicals and revolutionaries.

The *Observer* published a list of heretical statements alleged to have appeared in the *Boston Pilot*. Donahoe eventually printed an admission that he was responsible for what was printed in the *Boston Pilot* and that some of its more recent utterances might have exceeded the bounds of Catholic orthodoxy. Regardless of Donahoe's admission, the *Boston Pilot's* editorial policy remained adamantly nationalistic (Joyce, 1976).

Donahoe hired Patrick Lynch to edit the *Boston Pilot* in 1848. Lynch advocated an aggressive policy of republican nationalism for Ireland. Though he agreed with McGee, he approached the argument with moderation. He observed that while clerics did not agree with the political ideas of the Young Irelanders despite their guarantees of freedom of religion, and that while parish pastors did not think it was a good idea to challenge England, the clergy closest to the Irish peasants did favor the revolutionary movement. Lynch thought the Irish clergy were evenly divided on the question. Later Lynch roasted McMaster of the *Freeman's Journal* for criticizing a German republican leader and advocating monarchical and aristocratic forms of government. Lynch acidly observed that there is no "lower form of being than a blasphemer of liberty in a republic" (Joyce, 1976, p. 57).

Reverend John Roddan followed Lynch as editor of the *Boston Pilot* (1849–1858). It was under Roddan's guidance that the *Boston Pilot* started the growth that was to give it the highest circulation and the great national influence it enjoyed as the foremost Irish American journal of the 1870s. Roddan regarded the revolutionary Irish nationalists with outright hostility. He had bitter exchanges with Patrick Lynch, who was then a writer and co-proprietor of the *Irish-American*. Roddan regarded Lynch's earlier editorial policy in favor of the European republicans as mischievous. He portrayed Lynch as sympathetic to red republicans, whom Roddan described as murdering tyrants. Roddan described the *Irish-American* newspaper as having "wind, froth, bombast, bad taste, worse sense, radicalism, red republicanism, and atheistical tendencies" (Joyce, 1976, p. 58). Lynch countered by attacking McMaster's well-known dislike for Irish nationalists and rebuked McMaster as an implacable enemy of Irish Americans who hated the fatherland and freedom and downgraded the importance of the homeland to Irish immigrants (Joyce, 1976).

Even as the Irish were battling the fight they brought with them from Ireland, the Germans were doing the same thing. It seemed that most of the German American editors of newspapers wanted to support the revival of a revolution in Germany to make it a republic, but how and with what funds seemed to be the major argument. Gottfried Kinkel, a poet and former professor at Bonn in 1848, made a dramatic escape from Germany and migrated to America. He toured about to raise money for the German National Loan. This company would sell bonds to finance another revolution. In St. Louis, Carl Dänzer was editor of the German American newspaper *Anzeiger des Westens*. Through the pages of the newspaper, Kinkel's plans were described as impractical with a public debate arguing against Kinkel's ideas. His rival was Amand Gögg, a member of the red republicans. Gögg was attempting to raise funds for a German émigré colony in London to found a Revolutionary League (Wittke, 1957).

The battle between the supporters of Gögg and Kinkel became bitter and was fought through the German-language press. Editors took sides with sharp and coarse newspaper invective. This newspaper war revealed a sharp division between the older German leadership and the newer arrivals who had just entered the field of journalism. Papers like the *Westbote* of Columbus, Ohio; *New Yorker Staatszeitung*; and *Anzeiger des Westens* of St. Louis washed hands of both factions. Charges and counter-charges about alleged misappropriation of funds went back and forth in the German-language press throughout the 1850s (Wittke, 1957).

Earlier political infighting of the 1840s took place between Moritz Schoeffler of the Wisconsin *Banner* and Frederick Fratney of *Volksfreund*. Fratney, an Austrian political refugee, came from New York to be editor of *Volksfreund* in Wisconsin. Fratney did not like the tone of the newspaper, so he bought it at the end of 1847. Though he made the newspaper democratic, he remained at odds with the Wisconsin *Banner*. Fratney supported radical social causes such as land reform and his discourse was a biting anticlericalism, although his politics followed the straight Democratic Party line on most issues. Fratney and Schoeffler printed barbs against one another, which led to a split in what had been a unified German political front. Then in 1855, Fratney transferred his paper to Moritz Schoeffler and Fratney died. The paper was renamed *Banner und Volksfreund* (Wittke, 1957), united at last.

The Czechs were divided by their religious or philosophical differences as well. An example of this was in Chicago. By the 1920s there were four main Czech-language newspapers in Chicago: the *Narod* (Nation, founded 1894) served the Catholic community, *Svornost* (Concord, founded 1875) served the free-thinkers, *Spravedlnost* (Justice, founded 1900) served the socialists, and the *Denni Hlasatel* (Daily Herald, founded 1891) was a neutral paper for the larger midwestern Czech community (Gottfried, 1962).

Hungarian American editors spent much of their time and effort in pursuing personal squabbles and vendettas and in fighting "bloody" battles with various rival editors. The Hungarian American editors also fought the rivalries of two largest Hungarian American communities: Cleveland and New York. During these rivalries, if one paper espoused a cause, the other would oppose it or come up with an alternative solution.

Yiddish newspapers were not beyond the rivalries described in other ethnic newspapers. In 1897, the Arbeter Tsaytung Publishing Association had a split in their membership. One group, the minority group, began publishing the newspaper *Forverts* on New York's Lower East Side. The majority group remained with the Publishing Association and published *Abend Blatt*. The split in newspapers simply emphasized a larger rebellion within the Socialist Labor Party against Daniel De Leon's leadership and trade-union strategy. Within the Arbeter Tsaytung Publishing Association the feud was about social-democracy versus American commerce, about being motivated not by democratic concerns but by personal ambitions. Control of the newspaper was desired because whereas the majority side's approach to journalism was not liked by the minority, the minority side was thought to have become intoxicated by Hearst and Pulitzer-style yellow journalism and wanted to transform the newspaper into those images (Michels, 2000).

Even with all the fighting and shouting through the newspaper pages, ultimately the minority faction won. The minority leader was Abraham Cahan, who turned the *Forverts* newspaper

into the most popular Yiddish daily and among the most popular
ethnic newspapers in the United States. *Forverts* and its publishing association wielded greater influence than the Arbeter Tsaytung Publishing Association ever did in the 1890s (Michels,
2000). Another example of internal fighting created the newspaper *Der Blatt*, established in 2000 in New York after a succession
fight in the Satmar community, a large and influential Hasidic
community. At the death of Rabbe Moshi, the leadership was
split between sons, Aaron Teitelbaum and Zalman Lieb Teitelbaum. The original newspaper of the Satmar community, *Der
Yid*, went with the Zalman followers. Founded by Aharon Ros-
marin with editor Uriel Zimmer, *Der Yid* was bought by the
Satmar community and edited by Alexander Deutsch (Sender
Dietch), the executive vice president of the Council of Elders of
Satmar. The Aaron followers created the newspaper *Der Blatt* for
communication and public relations.

The Polish-language press also had its rivalries. When the
dominant Polish-language newspaper, *Kuryer Polski* in Milwaukee, criticized clerical meddling in politics, the church countered
by establishing a rival newspaper. The publisher, Michael
Kruszka, attacked the construction of a church because of the
huge debt it would place on the working-class parishioners.
Kruszka also supported Polish-language instruction in the parish
school's curriculum. The clergy was against him on both issues;
they wanted a church and wanted Polish language in the parish
schools. Though the church published two rival newspapers—the
Sowo (the Word) and *Dziennik Milwaucki* (Milwaukee's Daily)—
both failed within months of publication (Olszyk, 1940).

In 1906, other opponents of *Kuryer Polski* published *Nowiny
Polskie* under the editorship of Reverend Bolesaw Goral. Soon
the rivalry between *Kuryer Polski* and *Nowiny Polskie* split Milwaukee's Polish community into two antagonistic factions. On
February 11, 1912, Milwaukee's Archbishop Messmer issued an
edict urging the faithful not to read *Kuryer Polski*. Disobedience
of the decree could result in excommunication (Olszyk, 1940).
The next day, the Kuryer Publishing Company organized a dem-
onstration of more than 25,000 opponents of Messmer's edict.
Kruszka also established the fraternal insurance society, Federation of Poles in America, to counter both clerical sponsored asso-

ciations and the Polish National Alliance (PNA). The PNA earned Kruszka's wrath by its refusal to side with *Kuryer Polski* during the dispute with the church. The Federation of Poles in America continues to provide insurance coverage as Federation Life Insurance with its headquarters in Milwaukee. The Polish Roman Catholic Union filed a lawsuit against *Kuryer Polski* in 1918. In that same year, a few months before Poland's rebirth, Kruszka died. *Kuryer Polski* suspended publication in 1962 after the Internal Revenue Service declared the company delinquent on its taxes (Olszyk, 1940).

Summary

Internal problems were not the only problems for the ethnic newspaper editors, writers, and publishers. The rivalries and competition to produce a newspaper were often exacerbated by the isolation and alienation of the new immigrant in America. Some ethnic groups were beaten down by the struggle to have a better life. This long struggle left the Irish identifying themselves as an embattled and downtrodden minority even decades after they had complete control over the city's government. The impact these long struggles had on the ethnic communities often was not recorded. Tensions within the community often were a result of the differences generated by politics and religion in a place where the immigrants thought there would be no problems as they continued their search for that elusive American Dream.

Chapter Ten /
Cultural Pluralism

Never doubt that a small group of thoughtful,
committed citizens can change the world.
Indeed, it is the only thing that ever has.
Margaret Mead (1901–1978)

Melting pot, as a term referring to American culture, was used in a play written by Israel Zangwill called *Melting Pot* produced on Broadway in New York in 1908. The term was used to describe assimilation: the process of taking many cultures, bringing them into the United States, and turning them into one culture: an American one. The term was used again in 1915. Immigrant employees working for Henry Ford were required to attend English school, where they learned to say, "I am a good American." In a pantomime that supposedly symbolized the spirit of the company, there was a great melting pot in the middle of the stage. A long column of immigrant students descended into the pot from backstage dressed in outlandish clothing and carrying signs proclaiming their home countries. At the same time, from either side of the pot, another stream of men emerged; each prosperously dressed in identical suits of clothing and each carrying a little American flag (Higham, 2002). Ford was known for his ultra-conservative views, and though this image is contrived, it highlights the extremes that some voices in the American society were using to create a proper American image.

As more immigrant communities attempted to maintain their culture and integrate into American life, the image of a melting pot was changed to a salad bowl. This image allowed the immigrant to keep the home country identity but still be a part of the American mixture. This salad bowl concept was supported by studies that found that individuals were more likely to seek out individuals and groups who shared characteristics the immigrant regarded as important. These characteristics included values, religion, language, occupation, social class, nationality, and ethnicity. Immigrants who came did not identify at first with ethnic or nationalist groupings. They were not German but Württembergers, Saxons, and Westphalians. They were not Italian but Neapolitans, Sicilians, Calabrians, and Genoese (Higham, 2002).

This salad bowl increased in size until by the beginning of the 21st century, nearly 10 percent of the U.S. population—26.3 million—was born in other countries. This large percentage of the American population had to make choices as to how they wanted to identify themselves within the American culture. Culture can be defined as the socially transmitted behavior patterns, arts, beliefs, institutions, and other products of human work and thought characteristic of a community or population.

With this definition of culture in mind, the immigrants either could assimilate fully into the social structures and cultural life of America, or could emphasize and market the home country culture so that acculturation takes place and a blending of cultures happens. This dual culture can be illustrated by some Jewish populations who have managed to keep their religion and traditions but work and socialize in the larger American culture. At more of the extreme, immigrants can choose to remain separate, as illustrated by the Amish, who have kept within their own ethnic enclaves and do not accept the American culture. Or the immigrants can be marginalized, as radicals often are, or classified as refugees, whose culture and traditions make it harder for them to assimilate, especially when they did not want to leave their countries but had to because of war or persecution, like the Hmong. When the Hmong first migrated to America after the Vietnam War, it took them an average of 15 years to begin to assimilate into the American culture. The average time for most other immigrant groups has been 2–3 years.

As immigrants choose how to define themselves within the American society, and as larger populations of ethnic groups have migrated into the United States, the concept of pluralism is introduced as a better way to discuss the various cultures making up the American society. Pluralism is a salad bowl of cultures. The pluralist approach assumes that the ethnic community is an integral part of the American society and that each ethnic culture, despite its distinct internal dynamics, contributes to society as a whole. This has been supported through the mainstreaming of different cultural expressions like food (Mexican, Thai, and Chinese restaurants), clothing (pashmina shawls and ponchos), language greetings (ciao, bonjour, and adios), art (reprints from the world art collection), and decorations (batiks and African wood carvings).

As demonstrated throughout this work, the process of making a choice often begins with media. Ethnic presses introduce immigrants to their new community, thus helping to break down their cultural and social isolation. However, after the immigrant integrates into American society through a process of acculturation, and the immigrant chooses to either assimilate or not into the American culture, do the ethnic media inhibit or promote the assimilation of immigrants into American society? Examples of how the process of acculturation is incorporated through the use of newspapers are described in this chapter.

Acculturation

Acculturation is the process of cognitive, attitudinal, and behavioral adaptation to a new cultural system (Kim, 1977). Viewed as a communication process, each and every act of communication between beings is an adaptative process. As an immigrant tries to cope with the new environment, interpersonal contact and mass media provide ways to learn about the new culture (Khan, 1992). Through mass communication, the immigrant learns about the socio-cultural system of the host country. In these messages, the contents convey social values, norms of behavior, and traditional perspectives for interpreting the environment. Information-oriented media (newspapers, magazines, and TV news) are better at acculturation than entertainment media (Kim, 1977). The acculturation function of mass communication is particularly significant during the initial phase of the immigrant's process of accepting America. During this phase, the immigrant may not have the competence to develop interpersonal relationships with native-born Americans because of language or cultural barriers. A natural tendency for the immigrant is to withdraw from direct interaction with individuals and to turn to mass media as an alternative means of finding out about the new culture (Khan, 1992).

People who tend to seek both formal and informal relationships with the host culture in social situations have a greater potential for and may actually achieve a higher level of acculturation. Media transmits culture from one generation to another and from native-born to immigrants by reflecting societal values, norms of behavior, and traditional perspectives for inter-

preting the environment (Khan, 1992). Under the rubric of acculturation there are two approaches: assimilation and cultural pluralism. Assimilation suggests that as groups come into contact,
they become similar to one another, even though the non-
dominant group changes most by becoming more similar to the
dominant group. In plural societies, this assimilation theory is
most relevant. Groups and individuals living together are confronted with the question: Is my cultural identity of value and to
be retained? How they answer that question puts them into one
of four categories of approach to the experience: integration,
assimilation, separation/segregation, or marginalization (Berry,
Kim, Power, Young & Bujak, 1989).

Integration

Integration refers to when individuals want to maintain
their identity and at the same time become part of the larger societal framework. The Polish and Lithuanians wanted to have a
dual identity as ethnic and American. The ordination of Reverend Paul Rhode as a Roman Catholic bishop in 1908 symbolized
a permanent Roman Catholic recognition for the Poles and was
widely celebrated in Chicago (Green, 1975).

Many immigrant groups have wanted to create an identity
within the American society and have done so by celebrating a
saint's day. The immigrant group would use their home country
culture as a basis for deciding which dates to celebrate. For example, the Scottish celebrate St. Andrew's Day on November 30,
Hungarians celebrate St. Stephen's Day on August 20, the Welsh
celebrate St. David's Day on March 1, the English celebrate St.
George's Day on April 23, and the Irish celebrate St. Patrick's
Day on March 17.

A Scottish man, John M. Duncan, attended a celebration of
St. Andrew's Day in New York. His account provides an insight
into the way Americans and Scots interacted. Expecting to dine
on barley kale, sheep's head and trotters, and haggis, he ended
up consuming an American meal that lacked even oatcakes.
When he mildly protested, his host insisted that American life
had changed their eating habits. When he had served haggis in
previous years, he said, the customers shouted to the waiter to
remove it. Even an American chef's attempt to improve the taste
by adding raisins had not worked. Duncan complained about the

diluted nationality and concluded that the whole dinner was a spoiled mixture of Yankeeism and land-of-cakeism. He left early (Szasz, 2000, p. 109). Duncan, however, missed a good many symbols by which American Scots kept their identity alive. The hotel was draped with Scottish flags and medallions, inside and out. The Scots wore broad blue-and-white collars. Bagpipes provided the musical background backed by a full American orchestra. The entertainment included the reading of Scottish poems and the obligatory round of toasts. The pipes, whiskey, poems, songs, accent, and foods all helped create the feeling of Scotland, even though they were in America (Szasz, 2000).

Conflict between dual identities was reflected in the ethnic newspapers' coverage of the Irish Easter Rising. Despite living thousands of miles away from the troubles in Ireland, and despite having lived in America for years, the Irish still were concerned about the fate of their home country, as illustrated by the Easter Rising coverage in 1916. News from Ireland was in every issue of the Irish American press; but Irish Americans also viewed themselves (and wanted others to view them) as Americans and felt an affinity with their new country. The *Irish World* attempted to educate its readers in American history and, at the same time, remind them of notable events in Irish history. Both the *Irish World* and the *Kentucky Irish American* tried to establish a link between American history and the events in Dublin. The Easter Rising was compared to the American Revolution, and the newspapers likened the signers of the proclamation from the provisional government of the Irish Republic to George Washington and the signers of the Declaration of Independence (Potter, 1960).

Apart from the church, the Irish American press became one of the few institutions that the Irish could turn to for guidance. Newspapers fostered Irish insecurities and ambitions and helped devise strategies, however conflicting, by which the Irish could achieve a degree of acceptance in the United States. The *Boston Pilot* advised its readers to acknowledge existing social hierarchies, embrace the respectability that Catholicism could confer, and seek accommodation with the established order. The *Irish World* challenged the status quo and exhorted its readers to seek solidarity with other subservient groups as a means of advancing the status of the Irish (Mulcrone, 2003).

Dual identities were also part of the German experience in America. In 1848, Johann Bernard Stallo, a Latin teacher and lawyer who had immigrated 10 years earlier, described the ambivalent feelings of Germans who were in the process of adapting to the New World:

> Being German-American is a very personal thing. We want and we find external independence here, a free middle-class way of life, uninhibited progress in industrial development, in short, political freedom. To this extent we are completely American. We build our houses the way Americans do, but inside there is a German hearth that glows. We wear an American hat, but under its brim German eyes peer forth from a German face. We love our wives with German fidelity. . . We live according to what is customary in America, but we hold dear our German customs and traditions. We speak English, but we think and feel in German. Our reason speaks with the words of an Anglo-American, but our hearts understand only our mother tongue. While our eyes are fixed on an American horizon, in our souls the dear old German sky arches upward. Our entire emotional lives are, in a word, German and anything that would satisfy our inner longing must appear in German attire. (Adams, 1931, ch. 11, para 4)

Assimilation

Assimilation, which tends to create the internal conflict described above by Stallo, implies that the immigrant relinquishes cultural identity and accepts the one held by the host country. By the mid-19th century the main work of easing the assimilation of the Irish into American society had been completed (Joyce, 1976; McMahon, 1987). The Irish American newspapers changed from being an immigrant press to being an ethnic press. From 1870, the newspapers reflected not the efforts of an immigrant group groping for identity but an ethnic group that had defined its place and identity (McMahon, 1987). The *Irish World* moved from its early radicalism into more of a middle-class newspaper. The success and vitality of the Irish American press must be attributed to the talent and strong character of Irish American editors who "had a tremendous influence on shaping Irish nationalist opinion and helping the Irish transform themselves from foreigners and immigrants to American citizens"(McMahon, 1987, p. 183).

Establishing identity and integrating into American culture was also part of the Italian immigrant experience. Italian-language editors chastised the Italian immigrants for behavior that brought shame upon the Italians. The editors entreated them to abjure the stiletto, rag picking, filth, begging, and the nursing of infants in public. Anxious to win respect of Americans, publishers espoused standards of bourgeois respectability to learn English, to become citizens, and to participate in politics. These editors supported the ideology of accommodation (Vecoli, 1983). Even the renowned Italian socialist Arturo Giovannitti, when he became editor of *Il Proletario*, began writing in English. In accord with such attempts to accommodate, *Zajedničar*, a publication of the Croatian Fraternal Union of the United States, has published in English and Croatian since 1904, in Pittsburgh, Pennsylvania. *Nordstjernan* (The North Star) published since 1872 for Swedish Americans, carried news about the wild frontier wars with Native Americans and discoveries made by Swedes in the early issues. Today the newspaper links Scandinavian organizations such as Swedish singers, heritage societies, and museums. The paper has published from the beginning in both English and Swedish, though much of its online content is user-generated through upload functions.[1]

An important Chinese American editor who was committed to assimilation was Ng Poon Chew, editor of *Chung Sai Yat Po* (China West Daily). Ng Poon Chew cut off his queue, was fluent in English, and was so respected inside and outside the Chinese community that he made 86 transcontinental speaking tours. He believed his newspaper had journalistic integrity during a time of yellow journalism and racism. "We run a conservative paper in every way. It is cleanly edited and our whole aim is to educate and elevate the Chinese people; to make them better citizens and better people" (Danky & Wiegand, 1998, p. 86).

By the end of the 19th century, many Americans believed immigrants either were not assimilating or were assimilating too quickly, like the Asians and the Jews. Education became the first organized effort to promote assimilation. Thus the issue of who was controlling the schools became a hot topic with the German-language press, Catholic presses, and other immigrant groups that maintained their own language schools. Assimilation was either taken for granted or viewed as inconceivable.

Separation

Separation refers to immigrants who have no desire to relate to the host society, but want to maintain their traditions and culture. The French Canadians, who migrated into the Northeast, remained aloof and did not want to be a part of the American culture. Neither did the Hungarians, who refused to learn English and who ultimately returned home. Anti-assimilationist pressures existed. There were strong residual loyalties to the home culture. These loyalties were deployed especially by clergy, ethnic leaders, politicians, and some parents and most grandparents, who were heavily invested in the maintenance of cultural solidarity. A modern example is *Predvestnik* (Forerunner) in western Massachusetts founded in 2004. The newspaper appeals to Russian-language evangelical Christian refugees who prefer news media in their own Russian language.

Often the ethnic press was used to discourage assimilation of immigrants. The newspapers were used by special interests for political and propaganda purposes. Financial instability of the newspapers made them easy targets of people who saw financial advantage to limiting an immigrant to having the ethnic press as the sole source of information. The U.S. government believed that the ethnic press exerted a greater influence upon its readers than an English-language newspaper because of language and educational limitations and a report made to Congress suggested that the subsidization and domination of the ethnic press was proportionately more vicious in its effects than similar practices would be in the case of English newspapers (Kistler, 1960). The report confirmed that newspapers were important to assimilation and should continue so that all people could have a voice in the political makeup of the country. The report recommended that legislation should be introduced to control and to regulate the printing of foreign-language publications in the United States.

Marginalization

Marginalization is characterized by loss of contact with both the dominant group and the traditional one. This process can be exacerbated by maintaining the home country language and not learning English. An immigrant writer described this painful feeling of having language be a barrier and creating a sense of cultural emptiness. The writer referred to this as being in a cultural desert. "You try to look ahead but see no destination, you try to turn back but can't retrace your footsteps, and you end up drifting aimlessly without direction" (Zhou & Cai, 2002, p. 437).

This cultural distance creates more problems when trying to establish and maintain a harmonious relationship. This distance derives from differences in values.

> Interactions between members of societies diametrically opposed on core issues can quickly descend into rancor and hostility. For example, the lower standing of women in some societies attracts condemnation in cultures that value non-discriminatory gender relations. Conversely, members of male-dominated societies regard the occupational and sexual independence of Western women as repugnant and offensive. The most potent source of friction stems from differences in religious beliefs and practices. (Bochner, 1982, p. 46)

Process of Assimilation

Changes in U.S. immigration policy, which ended the Great Wave of immigration into the United States in 1924, were favorable to assimilation. First, the changes lessened the pressures on an immigrant to join the American mainstream since the immigrant was not being pushed by other immigrants coming into the United States. Second, immigrants as sojourners realized that they could no longer come and go with the expectation that they could reenter the United States. Many realized that their future was in the new society. A notable result was that the tenements thinned and new immigrants and their children moved rapidly toward the mainstream of American society (Graham, 2004).

Americanization included adding words to the home country language and adding other cultural elements to American life. Significant problems of assimilation and adjustment were more easily solved when at least some behavioral patterns of everyday life could be retained, such as shopping at a baker or butcher and enjoying a drink in a tavern. Americanization meant changing names, embracing the public schools, moving out of ethnic ghettos, and intermarrying. A survey of children of Polish immigrants in the mid-1920s found that most preferred American to Polish American as an identity. Many minority language speakers who participated in World War II found themselves stigmatized by other soldiers as dumb, backward, and underdeveloped. When they returned after the war, they hid their ethnic heritage and tried to forget their home country language. French was no longer used in the Midwest.

This process of Americanization was easier for the European immigrants, more difficult for Asians and Hispanics, and extremely difficult for Caribbean immigrants with African heritage (Graham, 2004). However, within this process, new immigrants caused the people who were American born but descended from the same home country to feel pushed aside and excluded, strangers in their own land. Some of them even perceived the new immigrants as a threat and a potential for un-Americanizing Americans (Horton, 1992; Zhou & Cai, 2002).

Role of Media

Ethnic presses supplement mainstream media and can acculturate non-English-speaking immigrants. Ethnic presses fill needs for the new immigrant that cannot be met by mainstream media and can promote and reinforce the upward mobility goal of the immigrant community: chasing the American Dream.

Values are reinforced through the ethnic press. Educational achievement and financial success is a value stressed by many ethnic presses, including the Chinese-language media. For example, a high-school senior in Los Angeles Chinatown said, "My father always read aloud news reports on winners of something, anything. When he did that, my whole body got stiffened. I felt he was talking to me and expecting me to do the same" (Zhou & Cai, 2002, p. 436). Another example is of a Chinese immigrant who moved to Washington, D.C., to take a high paying job in an accounting firm while maintaining his own business as a tax consultant. He ran a continuous advertisement in the local Chinese-language newspaper about his business even though he did not intend to expand it. "He said the purpose was not to get new business but to make a statement about you. It was important to show that you exist and that people know about you" (Zhou & Cai, 2002, p. 436).

Ethnic presses can influence certain habits, ways, and behaviors typically not found in the home country. Most immigrants are not familiar with how democracy works. Ethnic presses provide the immigrant with an outlet where he or she can write or call to voice an opinion—thus practicing democracy and causing a behavioral change. Immigrants depend on media to interpret politics; therefore, editors and publishers enjoy a significant influence on immigrant groups. These ethnic press leaders help shape their immigrant communities into cohesive groups by supporting immigrant interests and voicing claims, just as others have done in the past.

There have been editors who viewed their mission as one to assimilate their readers into the American mainstream. One such editor was James V. Donnaruma, who edited *La Gazzetta del Massachusetts* (1905–1930), an Italian-language newspaper in Boston. Donnaruma wanted to reform Italian immigrant behavior and thought that he could lead them on the way to Americanization (Deschamps & Luconi, 2002). He advised his readers to forget their old country manners and to honor their adopted land. He was on the side of the Bostonian establishment. Breaking the rules of ethnic loyalty, and alienating himself from the Italian community, he wanted to show his allegiance to American authorities and to the powerful Massachusetts Republicans, who contributed through advertising to the income of his newspaper (Deschamps & Luconi, 2002).

Ethnic newspapers sought acceptance by mainstream newspapers. For example, the *Boston Pilot* monitored the mainstream press for even the faintest signs of affirmation. Characterizing it as an indirect compliment, the *Boston Pilot* reprinted the following account from the *Chicago Tribune* about how the normally quarrelsome Irish uncharacteristically had failed to disrupt a Fourth of July gathering: "The attendance was almost entirely Irish, yet shillelagh encounters, nose and ear cannibalism, and broken whiskey glasses must be entirely unassociated with the occasion" (*Boston Pilot*, 1871 July 22, p. 4).[2]

The ethnic press can be both a help and a hindrance to Americanization. One objective is to recognize and foster a group consciousness among its readers and to preserve the language and culture of immigrant communities for as long as possible. Another objective is to perpetuate old-country rivalries and political disputes within the United States. These newspapers have made the transition easier for the immigrants to move from the old culture to the new culture through language and familiar customs such as using poetry and sentimental fiction, as seen in the belle-lettres (Wittke, 1957).

Cultural Pluralism

Cultural pluralism suggests that individuals and groups having different cultural identities could live together harmoniously and could be conducive to cultural exchange. Cultural pluralism totally rejects the melting pot hypothesis and supports the idea that ethnic groups can preserve their language, culture, institutions, and religion while still participating in American systems through the use of English. An example would be the Jewish immigrants, who wanted to belong, to fit into American society, but the price to belong was to divest past culture and tradition in order to accept the American culture. So, the Jews learned duality. They learned to be both authentically Jewish and unqualifiedly American at the same time. The key was education. Jewish publications in America did their part to strengthen identity, defend against outside forces, and assist in accommodating to life in America while discussing issues troubling the community (Reed, 1995).

Critics of cultural pluralism suggest that language must be left behind when participating at higher political levels. These critics also suggest that subcultures have no choice but either to assimilate into the dominant culture or to be marginalized, with all the negative political and economic consequences this entails. Critics also suggest that the cultural sphere cannot be separated from the economic and political spheres, especially in highly integrated consumer societies, where culture itself is commodified and can be used by politicians to manipulate the population. And finally, there is the tendency to conform to the norm, a norm which can only be a single and dominant culture and language.

Opposition between a strategy of integration and one of pluralism has been described by John Higham in his book *Strangers in the Land: Patterns of American Nativism* and is illustrated with the table below, synthesizing Higham's work (2002, pp. 112–120).

Integration	Pluralism
Eliminates ethnic boundaries	Maintains ethnic boundaries
Identifies community as big, includes all of human-kind	Identifies community as little, rooted in the past
Expresses the universalism of the Enlightenment	Rests on the diversitarian premises of romantic thought
Claims to be true champion of democracy	Claims to be true champion of democracy
Believes in majority rights	Believes in minority rights
Encourages conformity	Resists conformity—builds coalitions between groups
Maintains that democracy is equality of the individual	Maintains that democracy is an equality of groups
Social unit is individual right to self-definition, therefore assimilationist	Persistence and vitality of the group comes first. Individuals can only realize themselves through groups that nourish them
Stresses a unifying ideology	Guards a distinctive memory

As a critic, both positions—integration and pluralism—are unrealistic for several reasons. First, the positions assume a rigid, fixed ethnic group commitment that American life does not permit. Second, ethnic groups may be split along religious, class, and political lines and are not just one big group. More importantly, these positions of integration and pluralism are morally objectionable when an individual is asked to reject one's origins and to make being a success an indication of disloyalty to the home country and a way of being acculturated into a new society. These positions also limit the more autonomous and adventurous members of the society and sacrifices either the group for the individual or the individual for the group. Either way, someone loses.

Summary

Debate over the choices an immigrant has to make regarding culture is really a debate between unity and liberty. Some scholars interpret unity to mean coercion, while others regard diversity as little more than a disguise for fragmentation and disorder. The magnet drawing immigrants to America has been the fact that America has one of the world's highest standards of living, social acceptance, and mobility. And within this American society, the forces of assimilation are stronger than those of national or cultural separation. Do the ethnic presses inhibit or promote the assimilation of immigrants into American society? There are examples of ethnic presses inhibiting assimilation with strong nationalist sentiments and with keeping immigrants isolated within the ethnic enclave. However, there are also examples of ethnic presses promoting assimilation, reminding immigrants that to chase the American Dream, one must be an American.

[1] See www.nordstjernan.com.
[2] Retrieved from http://catalog.mwa.org of Newsbank and the American Antiquarian Society.

Chapter Eleven /
Future Unfolds

Dèyè mòn, gen mòn—
Behind every mountain is another mountain.
Haitian proverb

This Haitian proverb suggests that for each wave of immigrants entering the United States, the immigrants encounter many of the same problems faced by those who came before them. Furthermore, the proverb addresses the fact that more immigrants will follow. The choices these immigrants must make still exist and reflect how each wave wants to chase their version of the American Dream. Some contemporary immigrants feel that having a safe environment for them and their families is enough, after war has disrupted their lives. Others feel that being able to take advantage of social services and unskilled, low paying jobs is enough, even though the system is flawed. And some want to earn money to send back home. A 22-year-old immigrant works at a fast-food restaurant in the southern United States and makes $400 a week. She pays $100 to her sister for lodging and food, and sends $300 to her two sisters back home who are studying to be nurses. It is more than she could make in a month if she lived at home.

To achieve the American Dream, an immigrant must do three things: remember the past, look to the future, and hope that whatever happens in America will be a good thing. The process of moving into the American mainstream can be fast for some immigrants and slow for others. Educated and skilled immigrants move quickly into high paying jobs and homes in suburbs. Less educated and unskilled workers struggle to find jobs and affordable housing. Nevertheless, those who struggle still manage to send remittances, in the hundreds of thousands of dollars, back home to families for housing and education. Immigrants coming to America in the 21st century do so for many of the same reasons immigrants have come for the past two centuries. They come for a better future and better job prospects. They come to escape civil war in their country, or political persecution, or persecution for their religious beliefs. Not much has changed in the world. There is a change in immigration patterns since the recession of 2009. Remittances are reduced. The sojourner immigrants are returning home in large numbers. More refugees are being resettled in Europe than in the United States.

Larger Socio-Cultural Realm

The economy has been the barometer for how Americans have treated immigrant populations. When the economy is good and there are plenty of jobs, the immigrants are accepted. When the economy is bad, Americans accuse the immigrants of taking jobs. These anti-immigrant sentiments can be exacerbated with differences in religion and politics as demonstrated through the backlash against Muslims after September 11th, and with any nationality, the United States may be politically opposed, like the North Koreans, or the Iraqis.

Functions of the Media

While the newspaper played a dominant role during the 19th and 20th centuries in providing information to the new immigrant, radio and television now play a more important role. Access to the Internet has also been important among more recent immigrants. The availability of newspapers online from all over the world limit the need to have language-specific newspapers within immigrant communities designed to link the immigrant with his or her home country. The website www. Vakarai.us is one of the most visited Lithuanian-language media websites in the United States, and the Lithuanian Online Daily is on Facebook. Broadcast media have taken on the role of integrating the immigrant into the community.

Media in the 21st century provide the new immigrants with information about their new society, covering everything from national politics to detailed legal advice on local and personal matters including naturalization. The media provide information about the ethnic community; interpret political, economic, social, and cultural developments according to the viewpoint of the editor or journalist; and articulate interests of the ethnic group to include both the new and old societies. In New York, *Urdu Times*, published by Pakistani Khali-ur-Rahman, has grown from the "cut and paste" days to one where 80 percent of the newspaper is prepared in Pakistan and then transmitted via the Internet to presses in the United States.

Newspapers designed for the second generation immigrant are printed in English with a page or two in the home country language. Articles in this type of newspaper not only give the news of the home country but do so in a cultural context. The *Sing Tao Daily* has created programs to stimulate circulation and readership such as editorial repositioning, opinion exchanges with readers, special supplements including property and job market information, and is promoting itself as being more contemporary and middle class.

Reasons Immigrants Come

Immigrants initially came to the United States through Ellis Island in New York and Angel Island in San Francisco. Now immigrants can enter through any major airport in the country or over the borders with Canada and Mexico. Though current immigration laws establish a quota for the number of people who can enter the United States in any given year, there are hundreds of thousands of people who enter the United States without documentation by crossing unguarded portions of the Mexican border. These immigrants typically pay a significant amount of money to have someone help them cross. Such undocumented immigrants are usually stuffed in vans and trucks or compartments in cars with no air to breathe, no food to eat, and no water. Undocumented immigrants from Asia have come in shipping cargo containers sealed with no escape, much less ventilation. All have paid large sums of money for the often deadly trip.

Many undocumented immigrants come as sojourners. They want to find jobs in America so that they can send money home for their families to have a house and to educate their children. They hope to return home wealthier people than when they left. They frequently find that to achieve those dreams, they must live in crowded apartments, take menial and unskilled jobs to avoid detection by immigration authorities, and surrender hope of reaching the American Dream of home, money, and security. Some undocumented immigrants are exploited by unscrupulous employers and forced to work long hours at low wages with no overtime pay. They are castigated by supervisors and shunned by native-born Americans. Many have been robbed since it is known that undocumented immigrants do not have access to banks, cannot deposit their earnings, and consequently must carry their money with them or leave it in their houses.

To stay the flow of undocumented immigrants into the country, vigilante groups patrol the U.S. borders. The threat of terrorists increases the harm to which undocumented immigrants might be subjected. English language classes—classes that are a great source of help to the recent immigrant, providing a form of protection through integration—are difficult to get into due to demand. Recent immigrants must also face battles to obtain access to social services, driver licenses, education, job prospects, increased gang activity in their communities, and availability of affordable housing.

Religious Freedom

At the beginning of U.S. history, the dominant religion was Protestant. Conflicts with Catholic or Jewish immigrants were numerous. The Moravians, Mormons, and Amish, among others created enclaves in which they could practice their religion without fear of attack. The Catholics simply endured marginalization until John F. Kennedy was elected president and Catholics gained entrance to mainstream America. Jews have created communities in which members may function in both mainstream American society and a culturally Jewish society. Despite these early conflicts and divisions, there are numerous religions practiced in America today. The largest include the Christian sects of Roman Catholics, Protestants, Orthodox, and Anglicans. In addition, there are Baha'is, Buddhists, Chinese folk religionists, Confucians, ethnic religionists, Hindus, Jains, Jews, Muslims, Parsees, Sikhs, Shintoists, and Spiritists, among many others which are religious, nonreligious, atheist, and agnostic.

Controversies surrounding religion and immigrants in America have escalated since the September 11, 2001, attacks on the United States. Suddenly the people who have been both Muslims and next door neighbors are redefined—usually by stereotypes associated with their religion.

Political Persecution

Many ethnic newspapers in America are staffed by editors and journalists who immigrated to escape political persecution in their home countries. These men, and a few women, did not leave their ideology at home; they brought it with them. In America they are free to write and profess whatever ideology they wish. Many of these more politically forthright newspapers, such as those created by immigrant populations from Ireland, Italy, and Lithuania, are distributed in the home country. Additionally, there are underground newspapers with political agendas that are published within the United States but distributed only in the home country. This is because printing is cheaper, technology is more readily available, and the risks of being shut down are much less in the United States than in many other countries.

Belles-Lettres

Literature grounded in ethnic settings and fraught with the problems immigrants are continuing to face in America are mainstays in ethnic media. The strong linkage that such literature provides between an immigrant population in the United States and their home country is evident in translations of Joseph Brodsky's poetry, Isabel Alende's novels, and Carlos Fuentes' essays. This linkage is also shown in the fact that the Chinese-language newspapers in the United States print, in serial form, Chinese authored novels before they are printed in Asia. Mainstream media have begun to cash in on this need for a literary link to the homeland. Some newspapers and magazines published within the United States also produce foreign-language editions. Spanish is the most common, but regional publications in Asian languages are becoming more and more common.

Internal Issues

Tensions within the ethnic communities remain ever-present. The forming of new communities that include both recent and established immigrants can create tensions. Sociocultural practices in the home country play a significant role in how the immigrants behave in the United States. For example, the following editorial illustrates how some community members may try to use intimidation and threats against the media for control like they did in the home country. In the issue dated August 3–9, 2005, *The Haitian Times* ran this editorial:

> *Threats to* Haitian Times *Will Never be Tolerated.* Part of the job of a newspaper is to write stories that sometimes may make people wince and feel uncomfortable....*The Haitian Times*, in its six years existence, has done many of these stories, and we take the position that it is part of our job. We set out to portray our community simply as it is. We don't embellish just as we don't tarnish. Lately, we've done a spate of stories on subjects that have made some people wince. There have been stories about the sorry state of affairs of the Haitian music industry and about child support and the dead-beat dad phenomenon sweeping the Haitian community. Somehow, these issues have gotten to the underbelly of our emerging community, prompting some people to issue veiled and not so oblique threats. In the last week, we've received a couple of telephone calls from people threatening to do us bodily damage if we continue writing about them or about their 'bosses,' as one caller put it on Aug. 1....We hope that we're protected here that people will think twice before carrying out their threats. But we can't be sure of anything. A Colombian journalist was gunned down in Queens about a decade ago for writing stories about the drug cartels. We will take all precautionary measures to protect our safety. We will not be intimidated. We also vow to continue to uphold the highest degree of journalistic integrity to ensure that we don't libel anyone and that our coverage is fair, accurate and balanced.[1]

Cultural Pluralism

When choosing to stay in the United States, immigrants must make choices about acculturation and how they handle its subcomponents of assimilation, integration, marginalization, and separation. Some of these choices are difficult particularly if the immigrant was driven from his or her home country. Similarly these choices become even more complicated if the immigrant, intending to return home to family, is prevented from doing so by renewed economic or political crises in his or her home country.

Each ethnic newspaper has addressed the assimilation and acculturation processes an immigrant goes through. Some newspapers are helpful in assimilating recent immigrants into American culture. Editors of these papers support becoming a citizen, learning English, and registering to vote. Ethnic newspapers in Florida encourage immigrants to become citizens, register to vote, and then to vote and make a difference in their own communities. As to acculturation, other newspapers challenge their readers to integrate but encourage their readership to maintain their native language and culture. The editors of these types of newspapers rely on cultural activities to tie the two communities—that of the homeland and America—together. Music events, parades, festivals, and school events are championed within the pages of the ethnic newspapers.

Conversely, some newspapers advocate marginalization or even separation. They remind the readers that a better, more habitable country will exist when the war is over or the economic crisis has passed. These newspapers offer hope to populations like the sojourners. However, they create a marginalized society focused wholly on the political reform advocated between their pages. These newspapers advocate marginalization by using sensational headlines and screaming articles to get the readers' attention. Death is shown in all its forms of mutilation and grotesqueness as a means to enhance the reader's awareness of the perceived seriousness of the situation.

In addition to the changing political and social functions of the ethnic newspapers, the business functions have also changed. The frequency of the newspapers has changed from dailies to weeklies to stay alive. Unfortunately, many are continuing to lose subscribers with the exception of Latino and Asian publications. In spite of these trends, second, third, and fourth generations of immigrants are finding new ways of utilizing ethnic media. They are publishing in English, developing electronic ways of distributing information to distinct populations at a cheaper cost, and offering immigrant populations a version of the news placed in a context that includes both home country and American cultural perspectives.

The Road Ahead

What are the ethnic newspapers focusing on in the 21st century? They are praising the immigrant entrepreneurs who have revitalized immigrant neighborhoods. This is because it is believed that the path to better wages for some immigrant groups has been through establishing family-run businesses. Praise from the newspaper encourages entrepreneurship and these businesses can then advertise in the newspapers. Some businesses use the newspaper to keep the community aware that they are successful. Others subsidize the newspaper to gain control of information flowing to the community about the local and home country issues, especially political issues. In any case, newspapers have become part of the business sector of the ethnic community and contribute to the community's economic base. In addition to integration within the ethnic business structures, the newspaper provides linkages within the greater society in which people buy, sell, work, and own businesses that cater to the ethnic community. The networking opportunities are significant. Thus the 21st century ethnic newspaper is also a means of sharing information locally. This can be seen as positive in that the newspaper places emphasis on building the local community; or it can be seen as negative because restricting information flow to the local level limits business growth and keeps the ethnic community separate from others.

In addition to facilitating public discourse within a local community, new ethnic newspapers also address certain social issues circulating within American society. These include the myths that immigrants take jobs from Americans and cause unemployment. To dispel the myths, the ethnic newspapers publish articles emphasizing that new immigrants create jobs with their purchasing power and with the new businesses they start. Articles on immigrants published in these newspapers remind readers that illegal immigrants also contribute to the economic base of the community through paying taxes that often contribute as much to the public coffers as to the benefits they receive. Ethnic newspapers often print data on this topic, reporting recently that undocumented immigrants pay about 46 percent as much in taxes as do natives, but use about 45 percent as much in services.

Regardless, one million immigrants enter the United States every year. This is fewer than the entering rate during the Great Migration period of 1890 to 1914. In 1910, about 14.7 percent of people residing in the United States were foreign-born. In the 21st century, 10 percent of people residing in the United States are foreign-born.

Summary

What then can we say about the people who came, wrote, edited, and published newspapers for the millions of immigrants who have come to America? What can be learned from their issues, campaigns, and discussions?

We can learn that people are different but that those differences can influence the society as a whole. We can learn that people do not leave everything behind. They bring their memories, religions, politics, and culture. We can learn that through discussions of issues, people can understand each other better and learn to live in the world together. We can learn that no matter how hard one tries, some things will never happen. Families will not be reunited, educational aspirations will not be met, dreams and hopes will be dashed and smashed by the effort it takes to survive, to live one's own version of the American Dream. Ethnic newspapers have helped to shape the American Dream. They assume the immigrant will have a safe place, the opportunity to work and send money home, and the ability to get an education.

The American Dream was realized by many people who were not native-born Americans. Their children and grandchildren hear the stories but have become so assimilated into the American culture that ethnic newspapers provide the only alternative view of their life and its socio-cultural context. These ethnic newspapers also address other means of "happily ever after," not just that of peaceful assimilation. These newspapers speak to a different American Dream, one that includes a free homeland— one that is democratic, successful, and conducive to returning home again.

Dèyè mòn, gen mòn.

[1] Used with permission by publisher Garry Pierre-Pierre, 2005, August 10.

Bibliography

Adams, J. T. (1931). *The epic of America* (2nd ed.). New York: Greenwood Press.

Adams, W. P., Reichmann, E. & Rippley, L. J. (1993). *The German-Americans: An ethnic experience.* Max Kade German-American Center. Retrieved from http://www-lib.iupui.edu/kade/adams/toc.html

Avrich, P. (1991). *Sacco and Vanzetti: The anarchist background.* Princeton, NJ: Princeton University Press.

Balys, J. P. (1976, Spring). The American Lithuanian press. *Lituanus, Lithuanian Quarterly Journal of Arts and Sciences, 22*(1). Retrieved from http://www.lituanus.org/1976/76_1_02.htm

Baumgartner, A. W. (1931). *Catholic journalism: A study of its development in the United States, 1789-1930.* New York: Columbia University Press.

Bekken, J. (1995). The first anarchist daily newspaper: The Chicagoer Arbeiter-Zeitung. *Anarchist Studies, 3*(1). Retrieved from http://www.lwbooks.co.uk/journals/anarchiststudies/archive/vol3no1.html#bekken

Belth, N. C. (1979). *A promise to keep: A narrative of American encounter with anti-Semitism.* New York: Times Books.

"Berger long a dynamo of the socialists." (1929, July 17). Retrieved from http://www.wisconsinhistory.org/turningpoints/search.asp?id=789

Berry, J. W., Kim, U., Power, S., Young, M., & Bujak, M. (1989). Acculturation attitudes in plural societies. *Applied Psychology: An International Review, 38,* 185–206.

Besecker-Kassab, C. (1992). *Immigrant use of political media in the United States: A case study of the Maronite Lebanese of south Florida.* (Doctoral dissertation, University of Miami). Retrieved from http://webcatalog.mdpls.org/ipac20/ipac.jsp?session=W2620151U123E.153441&profile=dial&uri=link=3100018~!1164420~!3100001~!3100002&aspect=subtab13&men

u=search&ri=1&source=~!horizon&term=Besecker-Kassab
%2C+Charlotte+Kay.&index=PAUTHOR

Blejwas, S. A. (1993, Spring). Stanislaw Osada: Immigrant nationalist. *Polish American Studies, 50*(1), 23–50.

Blondheim, M. (1997). *New lights, old letters, new land: Three immigrant Hebrew printers in 19th century America.* Mount Scopus: The Hebrew University of Jerusalem.

Bochner, S. (1982). *Cultures in contact: Studies in cross-cultural interaction.* International Series in Experimental Social Psychology. Oxford, Oxforshire; New York: Pergamon Press.

Briggs, V. M., Jr. (2001). American unionism and U.S. immigration policy. Center for Immigration Studies. *Faculty Publications—Human Resource Studies.* Retrieved from http://works.bepress.com/vernon_briggs/72

Buhle, P. (1989). The Yiddish poets of di yunge. In F. Rosemont (Ed.), *Arsenal: Surrealist subversion.* Chicago: Black Swan Press.

Cahan, A. (1969). *The education of Abraham Cahan.* L. Stein (Trans.). Philadelphia: The Jewish Publication Society of America.

Carroll, F. M. (1978). *American opinion and the Irish question, 1910–23: A study in opinion and policy.* Dublin; New York: Gill and Macmillan; St. Martin's Press.

"The Chinese in California." (1852, June 24). *The Farmers' Cabinet, 50*(46), 2. Retrieved from http://catalog.mwa.org of Newsbank and the American Antiquarian Society.

Clark, D. (1991). *Erin's heirs: Irish bonds of community.* Lexington, KY: University Press of Kentucky.

Cogley, J. (1972). *Catholic America.* New York: The Dial Press.

Conzen, K. N. (1976). *Immigrant Milwaukee, 1836-1860: Accommodation and community in a frontier city.* Harvard Studies in Urban History. Cambridge, MA: Harvard University Press.

Cozine, A. (2004). Czechs and Bohemians. *Encyclopedia of Chicago.* Retrieved from http://www.encyclopedia.chicagohistory.org/pages/153.html

Cullen, J. (2003). *The American dream: A short history of an idea that shaped a nation.* Oxford; New York: Oxford University Press.

Danky, J. P. & Wiegand, W. A. (1998). *Print culture in a diverse America. History of communication.* Urbana, IL: University of Illinois Press.

David, H. (1963). *The history of the haymarket affair: A study of the American social-revolutionary and labor movements* (3rd ed.). New York: Collier Books.

Deschamps, B. & Luconi, S. (2002, Summer). The publisher of the foreign-language press as an ethnic leader? The case of James V. Donnaruma and Boston's Italian-American community in the interwar years. *The Historical Journal of Massachusetts, 30*(2), 126–143.

Desmond, H. J. (1969). *The A.P.A. movement.* New York: Arno Press.

Doone, F. P. (1902). *Observations by Mr. Dooley.* Retrieved from http://www.gutenberg.org/etext/4729

Fishman, J. A. & Nahimy, V. (1966). The ethnic group school and mother tongue maintenance. In J. A. Fishman (Ed.), *Language loyalty in the United States; the maintenance and perpetuation of non-English mother tongues by American ethnic and religious groups* (pp. 92–126). The Hague: Mouton.

Foik, P. J. (1930/1969). *Pioneer Catholic journalism.* United States Catholic Historical Society. [Monograph series]. London: Greenwood Press.

Gabaccia, D. (1988). *Militants and migrants: Rural Sicilians become American workers.* New Brunswick, NJ: Rutgers University Press.

Gottfried, A. (1962). *Boss Cermak of Chicago: A study in political leadership.* Seattle: University of Washington Press.

Graham, O. L. (2004). *Unguarded gates: A history of America's immigration crisis.* Lanham, MD: Rowman & Littlefield.

Green, V. R. (1975). *For God and country: The rise of Polish and Lithuanian ethnic consciousness in America, 1860-1910.* Madison: State Historical Society of Wisconsin.

Guillory, D. (1985, July 3). The plain people: A portrait of the Illinois Amish. *Illinois Times,* pp. 4–9.

Habermas, J. (1974). The public sphere. *New German Critique, 1*(3), 49.

Handlin, O. (1970). *Boston's immigrants, 1790-1880: A study in acculturation.* New York: Atheneum.

Harris, R. & Jacobs, D. (Eds.). (1989). *The search for missing friends, Irish immigrant advertisements placed in the* Boston Pilot (3 vols.). Boston: New England Historic Genealogical Society.

Hays, S. P. (1957/1995). *The response to industrialism, 1885-1914.* Chicago: University of Chicago Press.

Henritze, B. K. (1995). *Bibliographic checklist of African American newspapers.* Baltimore, *MD:* Genealogical Publishing.

Herbert, B. (2005). *Promises betrayed: Waking up from the American dream.* New York: Times Books.

Higham, J. (2002). *Strangers in the land: Patterns of American nativism, 1860-1925.* New Brunswick, NJ: Rutgers University Press.

Hoerder, D. & Harzig, C. (1987). *The immigrant labor press in North America, 1840s-1970s: An annotated bibliography.* New York: Greenwood Press.

Horton, J. (1992). The politics of diversity in Monterey Park, California. In L. Lamphore (Ed.), *Structuring diversity* (pp. 215–245). Chicago: University of Chicago Press.

Hosokawa, B. (1998, April). The sentinel story. *Peace & Change, 23*(2), 135–148.

Hosokawa, B. & Noel, T. (1998). *Out of the frying pan: Reflections of a Japanese American.* Boulder, CO: University Press of Colorado.

Hunter, E. (1960). *In many voices; our fabulous foreign-language press.* Norman Park, GA: Norman College.

Huntzicker, W. (1995). Newspaper representation of China and Chinese Americans. In F. Hutton & B. S. Reed (Eds.), *Outsiders in 19th century press history: Multicultural perspectives* (pp. 93–114). Bowling Green, OH: Bowling Green State University Popular Press.

Jacoby, T. (2004). *Reinventing the melting pot: The new immigrants and what it means to be American.* New York: Basic Books.

Jillson, C. C. (2004). *Pursuing the American dream: Opportunity and exclusion over four centuries, American political thought.* Lawrence, KS: University Press of Kansas.

Joshi, A. (1999, December 27). *Whenever autumn arrives. Connect!* Retrieved from http://www.sawf.org/newedit/edit122799/index.asp

Joyce, W. L. (1976). *Editors and ethnicity: A history of the Irish-American press, 1848-1883. The Irish-Americans.* New York: Arno Press.

Kenny, K. (1995). The Molly Maguires and the Catholic church. *Labor History, 36*(3), 345–376.

Kenworthy, T. (2004, November 29). Hmong get closer look since shootings. *USA Today.* Retrieved from http://www.usa today.com/news/nation/2004-11-29-hmong-closerlook_x.htm

Khan, M. A. (1992). Communication patterns of sojourners in the process of acculturation. *The Journal of Development Communication, 3*(2), 65–73.

Killebrew, M. (2005). *I never died. The words, music and influence of Joe Hill.* Retrieved from http://www.kued.org /productions/joehill/voices/article.html

Kim, Y. Y. (1977). Communication patterns of foreign immigrants in the process of acculturation. *Human Communication Research, 4,* 66–67.

Kinzer, D. L. (1964). *An episode in anti-Catholicism: The American protective association.* Seattle: University of Washington Press.

Kistler, M. O. (1960, September). The German language press in Michigan. *Michigan History, 44,* 303–323.

Kloss, H. (1966). German-American language maintenance efforts. In J. A. Fishman (Ed.), *Language loyalty in the United States* (pp. 206–252). The Hague: Mouton.

Kwitchen, M. A. & McMaster, J. A. (1949). *A study in American thought.* Washington, DC: The Catholic University of America Press.

Lai, H. M. (1987). *The Ethnic Press in the United States: A Historical Analysis and Handbook* (pp. 27-43). Westport, CT: Greenwood Press.

Laguerre, M. S. (1998). *Diasporic citizenship: Haitian Americans in transnational America.* New York: Macmillan.

Lee, L. T. (1988). *Early Chinese immigrant societies: Case studies from North America and British Southeast Asia. Asian studies series.* Singapore: Heinemann Asia.

Levinson, J. (2004, Spring/Summer). Modernism from below: Moyshe-Leyb Halpern and the situation of Yiddish poetry. *Jewish Social Studies, 10*(3), 143–160.

Levitas, D. (1999). The history of anti-Semitism in the United States. *Groliers Multimedia Encyclopedia*. Retrieved from http://books.google.com/books?id=ST60t-8BsxoC&pg=PA33& lpg=PA33&dq=Levitas,+D.++The+history+of+anti-Semitism +in+the+United+States.&source=bl&ots=gCucaQfPYF&sig= UpCVAvy-t1GFLo-tGq8ENBaqAIs&hl=en&ei=Dxs5S4z9M4i WtgfHlvT9CA&sa=X&oi=book_result&ct=result&resnum=8& ved=0CBwQ6AEwBw#v=onepage&q=Levitas%2C%20D.%20 %20The%20history%20of%20anti-Semitism%20in%20the% 20United%20States.&f=false

Liptak, D. A. (1989). *Immigrants and their church, makers of the Catholic community*. New York; London: Macmillan.

Lovoll, O. S. (1977). Decorah-Posten: The story of an immigrant newspaper. *Norwegian-American Studies, 27*, 77–100.

Madison, C. A. (1976). *Jewish publishing in America: The impact of Jewish writing on American culture*. New York: Sanhedrin Press.

McCunn, R. L. (1979). *An illustrated history of the Chinese in America*. San Francisco: Design Enterprises.

McMahon, E. (1987). The Irish-American press. In S. Miller (Ed.), *The ethnic press in the United States: A historical analysis and handbook* (pp. 179–181). New York: Greenwood Press.

McManamin, F. G. (1976). *The American years of John Boyle O'Reilly, 1870-1890*. New York: Arno Press.

Mencken, H. L. (1949). *A Mencken chrestomathy: His own selection of the choicest writing*. New York: Random House.

Mendoza, L. A. (2009, September 27). *The hidden history of the U.S. Latino press*. Retrieved from http://axisoflogic.com/art man/publish/Article_57036.shtml

Michels, T. (2000). "Speaking to Moyshe": The early socialist Yiddish press and its readers. *Jewish History, 14*, 51–82.

Mitchel, J. (1876/1997). *Jail journal*. (Original ed.). Dublin: M.H. Gill; Santa Barbara, CA: Woodstock Books.

Mulcrone, M. (2003). The famine Irish and the Irish-American press: Strangers in a hostile land. *American Journalism, 20*(3), 49–72.

Murrin, J. M., Johnson, P. E., McPherson, J. M., Gerstle, G., Rosenberg, E. S. & Rosenberg, N. L. (2002). *Liberty, equality, power: A history of the American people.* (Vol. 2, Since 1863). Belmont, CA: Wadsworth.

Muzik, E. J. (1964). Victor L. Berger: Congress and the red scare. *Wisconsin Magazine of History, 47,* 309–318.

Nelson, B. C. (1992). Arbeiterpresse und arbeiterbewegung: Chicago's socialist and anarchist press, 1870-1900. In E. Shore, K. Fones-Wolf & J. P. Danky (Eds.), *The German-American radical press: The shaping of a left political culture, 1850-1940* (pp. 81–107). Urbana, IL: University of Illinois Press.

Nelson, V. J. (2006, July 4). Poul Andersen, 84; published nation's only Danish-language weekly paper. *The Los Angeles Times.* Retrieved from http://articles.latimes.com/2006/jul/04/local/me-andersen4

Norton, W. (1977). *Religious newspapers in the old northwest to 1861: A history, bibliography, and record of opinion.* Athens: Ohio University Press.

Ochs, E. (1986). Introduction. In B. B. Schieffelin & E. Ochs (Eds.), *Language socialization across cultures* (p. 1). Cambridge, UK: Cambridge University Press.

Olszyk, E. G. (1940). *The Polish press in America.* Milwaukee, WI: Marquette University Press.

Outcault, R. F. (1995, October). *R.F. Outcault's the yellow kid: A centennial celebration of the kid who started the comics.* Northampton, MA: Kitchen Sink Press.

Paine, A. B. (1904). *Th. Nast his period and his pictures.* New York: Harper & Brothers. Retrieved from http://books.google.com/books?id=2BwxAAAAMAAJ&pg=PR1&lpg=PR1&dq=th.+nast+his+period+and+his+pictures&source=bl&ots=RCkxu15Ywa&sig=RK0K85qLzUqe77tVCIXBIMRoQ0A&hl=en&ei=HPg4S4D1L4y1tgeTt4SQCQ&sa=X&oi=book_result&ct=result&resnum=1&ved=0CAsQ6AEwAA#v=onepage&q=&f=false

Paine, T. (1776). *Common sense.* Mount Vernon, NY: A. Colish.

Park, R. E. (1922). *The immigrant press and its control.* New York; London: Harper & Brothers.

Parks, A. W. (1995). *Sui Sin Far/Edith Maude Eaton: A literary biography, the Asian American experience.* Urbana, IL: University of Illinois Press.

Peck, G. (2000). *Reinventing free labor: Padrones and immigrant workers in the North American West, 1880-1930.* Cambridge, UK: Cambridge University Press.

Poore, C. (1992). The pioneer calendar of New York City: Chronicler of German-American socialism. In E. Shore, K. Fones-Wolf & J. P. Danky (Eds.), *The German-American radical press: The shaping of a left political culture, 1850-1940* (pp. 108–122). Urbana, IL; Chicago: University of Illinois Press.

Potter, G. W. (1960). *To the golden door; the story of the Irish in Ireland and America.* Boston: Little Brown.

Pückler-Muskau, H. & Austin, S. (1833). *Tour in England, Ireland, and France, in the years 1826, 1827, 1828, and 1829. With remarks on the manners and customs of the inhabitants, and anecdotes of distinguished public characters. In a series of letters.* Philadelphia: Carey, Lea & Blanchard.

Puskás, J. (1982). *From Hungary to the United States (1880-1914).* Budapest: Akadáemiai Kiadáo.

Puskás, J. (2000). *Ties that bind, ties that divide: 100 years of Hungarian experience in the United States, Ellis Island Series.* New York: Holmes & Meir.

Reed, B. S. (1995). Pioneer Jewish journalism. In F. Hutton & B. S. Reed (Eds.), *Outsiders in 19th century press history: Multicultural perspectives* (pp. 21-54). Bowling Green, OH: Bowling Green State University Popular Press.

Reiff, J. L. (2005). *The press and labor in the 1880s.* Retrieved from http://www.encyclopedia.chicagohistory.org/pages/11407_em.html

Riis, J. (1890). *How the other half lives: Studies among the tenements of New York.* New York: George Scribner's Sons.

Rippley, L. J. (1976). *The German-Americans.* Boston: Twayne.

Rodechko, J. P. (1970). An Irish-American journalist and Catholicism: Patrick Ford of the *Irish World. Church History, 39*(4), 524–540.

Rolle, A. F. (1999). *Westward the immigrants: Italian adventurers and colonists in an expanding America.* Niwot, CO: University Press of Colorado.

Roosevelt Off for West. (1917, September 21). *New York Times* (para. 2). Retrieved from http://query.nytimes.com/mem/archive-free/pdf?_r=1&res=9506E1DA103AE433A25752C2A96F9C946696D6CF

Rosdail, J. H. (1961). *The sloopers, their ancestry and posterity.* Broadview, IL: Photopress for the Norwegian Slooper Society of America.

Sandmeyer, E. C. (1939). *The anti-Chinese movement in California.* Urbana, IL: University of Illinois Press.

Schreiber, B. (1996). Return of the prodigal father and son. *Humanist, 56*(1), 47–48.

Schroeder, J. B. (1976). Wisconsin synod: Right or wrong in handling the Bennet Law? (Senior church history paper submitted in partial fulfillment of course requirements at WLS, Meqron, WI). Retrieved from http://www.wlsessays.net/files /SchroederBennett.pdf

Schurz, C. (1907). *Reminiscences.* (3 vols). New York: McClure Publishing.

Sengupta, S. (2001, October 29). Refugees at America's door find it closed after attacks. *The New York Times.* Retrieved from http://www.nytimes.com/2001/10/29/nyregion/29REFU.html

Sheridan, R. B. (1908). *The Critic* (Act I, Sc. 2, p. 9). Retrieved from http://book.google.com/books?id=0T4MAAAAMAAJ&dq= The+Critic+by+Richard+Sheridan&printsec=frontcover&sour ce=bl&ots+Ysi-9RTG16&sig=y163niZHFvJAsmDoEOxE5STE _Y4&ht=en&ei=FLw3S4r0J5G1tgferJ2RCQ&sa=X&oi=book _result&ct+result&resnum=3&ved=0CBMQ6AEwA g#v=onepage&q=&f=false

Simmons, C. A. (1998). Preface. *The African American press: A history of news coverage during national crises, with special reference to four black newspapers, 1827-1965* (pp. 1–4). Jefferson, NC: McFarland.

Sleeper, J. (1999). *Should American journalism make us Americans?* Cambridge, MA: The Joan Shorenstein Center on the Press, Politics and Public Policy. Retrieved from http:// www.hks.harvard.edu/presspol/publications/papers/discussio n_papers/d38_sleeper.pdf

Smith, M. L. (2003). *INS–US immigration & naturalization service history.* Retrieved from http://www.uscitizenship.info/ins- usimmigration-insoverview.html

Sonntag, M. (1994). Fighting everything German in Texas, 1917-1919. *Historian, 56*, 655–670.

Sung, B. L. (1971). *The story of the Chinese in America.* New York: Collier Books.

Szasz, F. M. (2000). *Scots in the North American West, 1790-1917.* Norman, OK: University of Oklahoma Press.

Várdy, S. B. (1985). *The Hungarian-Americans, the immigrant heritage of America series.* Boston: Twayne.

Várdy, S. B. & Várdy, A. H. (1989). *The Austro-Hungarian mind: At home and abroad.* New York: Columbia University Press.

Vecoli, R. J. (1983). The formation of Chicago's "Little Italies." *Journal of American Ethnic History, 2,* 5–20.

Viswanath, K. & Arora, P. (2000). Ethnic media in the United States: An essay on their role in integration, assimilation, and social control. *Mass Communication & Society, 3*(1), 39–56.

Vygotsky, L. S. (1978). *Mind in society: The development of higher psychological processes.* M. Cole, V. John-Steiner, S. Scribner & E. Souberman (Eds.). Cambridge, MA: Harvard University Press. Retrieved from http://books.google.com /books?hl=en&lr=&id=RxjjUefze_oC&oi=fnd&pg=PA1&dq=V ygotsky,+L.+S.+%26+Cole,+M.+(1978).+Mind+in+society:+Th e+development+of+higher+psychological+processes.+Cambri dge:+Harvard+University+Press.&ots=ofBWQZq1et&sig=co1 F1c-3uI1weDFMiqZQkwXoUx4#v=onepage&q=&f=false

Wilson, C. C. & Gutiérrez, F. (1985). *Minorities and media: Diversity and the end of mass communication.* Beverly Hills, CA: Sage.

Wittke, C. F. (1957). *The German-language press in America.* Lexington, KY: University of Kentucky Press.

Yin, X. (2003). Voices from the gold mountain. *World & I, 18*(2), 291–301.

Yokoi, I. (1993, September 19). "Little Tokyo - Extra! Extra! Rafu Shimpo Is 90." *The Los Angeles Times.* Retrieved from http:// articles.latimes.com/1993-09-19/news/ci-36906_1_rafu-shimpo

Zhou, M. (2002, February 22–23). *The enclave economy and ethnic social structures: Variations in neighborhood-based resources for immigrant adolescents in Los Angeles.* Paper presented at session III "Network as Context" of the Princeton Economic Sociology Conference on the U.S. Economy in Context, Princeton University.

Zhou, M. & Cai, G. (2002). Chinese language media in the United States: Immigration and assimilation in American life. *Qualitative Sociology*, *25*(3), 419–440.

Zubrzycki, J. (1958). The role of the foreign-language press in migrant integration. *Population Studies*, *12*(1), 73–82.

Index

D^T